Jacob of Sarug's Homily on the Sinful Woman

Texts from Christian Late Antiquity

33

Series Editor

George Anton Kiraz

TeCLA (Texts from Christian Late Antiquity) is a series presenting ancient Christian texts both in their original languages and with accompanying contemporary English translations.

Jacob of Sarug's Homily on the Sinful Woman

Metrical Homilies of Mar Jacob of Sarug

Translation and Introduction by
Scott Fitzgerald Johnson

gorgias press
2013

Gorgias Press LLC, 954 River Road, Piscataway, NJ, 08854, USA

www.gorgiaspress.com

Copyright © 2013 by Gorgias Press LLC

All rights reserved under International and Pan-American Copyright Conventions. No part of this publication may be reproduced, stored in a retrieval system or transmitted in any form or by any means, electronic, mechanical, photocopying, recording, scanning or otherwise without the prior written permission of Gorgias Press LLC.

2013

ISBN 978-1-61719-834-2   ISSN 1935-6846

Library of Congress Cataloging-in-Publication Data

A Cataloging-in-Publication Record is Available from the Library of Congress.

Printed in the United States of America

To Jack Tannous

Table of Contents

Table of Contents vii
Preface ix
Introduction 1
    I. The Sinful Woman in the Gospels..1
    II. The Sinful Woman in the Syriac Tradition 4
    III. Jacob of Sarug's *memra* on the Sinful Woman.....................6
    IV. Jacob and the Syriac Verse Tradition on the Sinful Woman 13
    V. Jacob and Romanos the Melode 15
    VI. Conclusion 23
Text and Translation..25
Appendix: Romanos and the Syriac Verse Tradition on the Sinful Woman 85
    I. Introduction..85
    II. Note on the Text of the Ephremic *memra* on the Sinful Woman ...86
    III. Romanos and the Ephremic *memra* on the Sinful Woman 88
    IV. Note on the Text of the *Soghitha* on the Sinful Woman and Satan 97
    V. Romanos and the *soghitha* on the Sinful Woman and Satan 98
    VI. Conclusion 110
Abbreviations 113
Works Cited...115
Index..125

Preface

The research contained in this little book extends back more than ten years, to a time when I wrote a M.Phil. dissertation at Oxford on Romanos the Melode and the Syriac tradition (2001), under the supervision of Prof. Averil Cameron. I decided to write my D.Phil thesis on a completely different topic, and the only visible fruit of that earlier work was the translation published in *Sobornost / Eastern Churches Review* in 2002 (24.1: 56–88) under the title "The Sinful Woman: A *memra* by Jacob of Serugh". (To the best of my knowledge, the first translation into a western language.) That translation is re-published here in a moderately revised form, though now with a facing-page Syriac text from the Bedjan edition. I am grateful to Father Stephen Platt and the editors of *Sobornost* for allowing me to present it in this new format. The introductions and annotations to the *Sobornost* article were meager by comparison to the analytical work that had inspired the translation to begin with. I am happy to be able to offer that work here, in a fully revised form. The Introduction and the Appendix on Romanos attempt to situate Jacob's *memra* in a broad literary history spanning the Greek and Syriac liturgical poetry of Late Antiquity. I would like to thank George Kiraz and Sebastian Brock for accepting this book as part of the excellent Homilies of Mar Jacob of Sarug series. I am grateful for Sebastian's careful reading of my translation and his suggestions for improvement. Any remaining errors or infelicities are my own responsibility. I would also like to thank Margaret Mullett and the research staff at Dumbarton Oaks for their commitment to a "big tent Byzantium" and for encouraging Syriac studies in particular. Likewise, I am grateful to my colleagues at Georgetown, in Classics, Arabic, and other departments, for supporting such a lively scholarly community. Adam McCollum of the Hill Museum and Manuscript Library very helpfully discussed this volume with me during its preparation. As always, I would like to thank my family and especially my wife, Carol, and our children, Susanna, Daniel and Thomas, for their love.

Finally, I would like to thank Jack Tannous, to whom I dedicate this modest book. Jack has encouraged my study of Syriac through his passion for the language and through a long friendship that extends back to our time in Oxford reading Syriac together at the Oriental Institute. Our brief sojourns in the same city, first at Oxford and then more recently in Washington, DC at Dumbarton Oaks, have been two of the most intellectually engaging times in my life. Jack is a dear friend, a sincere (and formidable) scholar, and a magnanimous teacher. I dedicate this book to him in gratitude for all those things and more.

Introduction

I. The Sinful Woman in the Gospels

The story of the woman who anointed and washed Jesus at a banquet is one of a small number of episodes that appear in all four Gospels (Matt 26:6–13; Mark 14:3–9; Luke 7:36–50; John 12:1–11).[1] In Matthew 26:6–13 she goes to the house of Simon the Leper in Bethany (ἐν Βηθανίᾳ ἐν οἰκίᾳ Σίμωνος τοῦ λεπροῦ) two days before the Passover to find Jesus and to anoint his head with costly perfume from an alabaster jar (ἀλάβαστρον μύρου). The disciples criticize this inexplicable "waste" of money (ἡ ἀπώλεια αὕτη), which could have been given to the poor, but they are rebuked by Jesus, who says, "By pouring this perfume (τὸ μύρον τοῦτο) on my body she has prepared me for burial (πρὸς τὸ ἐνταφιάσαι με). Truly I tell you, wherever this gospel is proclaimed in the whole world, what she has done will also be told in remembrance of her."[2] Immediately Judas Iscariot goes and strikes a deal with the chief priests, to deliver Jesus to them for 30 pieces of silver (26:14–16), but it is not Judas who questions the use of the perfume.

In Mark 14:3–9 the story is much the same, only it is not the disciples who criticize but just "some who became indignant in themselves" (ἦσαν δέ τινες ἀγανακτοῦντες πρὸς ἑαυτούς). Like the disciples in Matthew, these bystanders complain that the oil could have been sold for money. In Matthew it is just "a large sum" (πολλοῦ), but in Mark the figure is given as 300 denarii. Here, too, Judas seeks afterwards to betray Jesus (14:10–11), but there is no mention, however, of the sum Judas was paid to betray

---

[1] Two respected commentators on this scene conclude that all four episodes are narratively related: Bovon 2002 (s.vv. Luke 7:36–50) and Elliott 1974. Others have claimed that Luke's version is a separate story from the Matthew, Mark, and John: e.g. Legault 1954. In this study I follow Bovon and Elliott in seeing the four as "written fixations of a single gospel memory" (Bovon).

[2] All translations in this book are my own unless otherwise noted.

Jesus, nor is he connected at all to the questioning of the Sinful Woman's actions.

John 12:1–11 has Jesus dining at the house of Lazarus ("whom Jesus raised from the dead"), not Simon, six days before the Passover, not two, and the woman is called "Mary" (Μαριάμ). This Mary was identified in the West, at least from the time of Gregory the Great, with Mary Magdalene, out of whom Jesus cast seven devils in Luke 8:2, who was at the foot of the cross in Mark 15:40, and who came to the tomb on the third day in Matthew 28, Mark 16, Luke 24, and John 20.[3] In John, this Mary anoints Jesus' feet, not his head, and wipes them with her hair (ἐξέμαξεν ταῖς θριξὶν αὐτῆς τοὺς πόδας αὐτοῦ). Judas Iscariot criticizes Mary for what seems like a waste: "Why was this perfume not sold for 300 denarii and the money given to the poor?" Jesus rebukes him saying, "Leave her alone. She bought it so that she might keep it for the day of my burial (εἰς τὴν ἡμέραν τοῦ ἐνταφιασμοῦ μου). You always have the poor with you, but you do not always have me." Following this, the chief priests decide to kill Lazarus also when they kill Jesus (12:10–11), though Judas' involvement in the plot is not mentioned here.

In Luke 7:36–50 the story is remarkably expanded. The unnamed woman—called "a woman who was a sinner in the city" (γυνὴ ἥτις ἦν ἐν τῇ πόλει ἁμαρτωλός)—goes to the house of Simon the Pharisee, not the Leper, who has invited Jesus to dine with him (ὁ Φαρισαῖος ὁ καλέσας αὐτόν). The scene does not occur in Passover week at all and comes at a much earlier point in Jesus' ministry. Concerning the anointing, Luke 7:38 reads as follows:

> She stood behind him at his feet, weeping, and began to bathe his feet with her tears and to dry them with the hair of her head. And she was kissing his feet and anointing them with the perfume.

---

[3] See Benedicta Ward's summary of the western Christian literature on Mary Magdalene in Ward 1987, 10–25; and Szövérffy 1963. For the reception of Mary Magdalene in a broader cultural context, see Haskins 1993. The association of the Sinful Woman with Mary Magdalene has since been abandoned by the Roman Catholic Church (Cross and Livingstone 1997, 1049–1050). The eastern Christian tradition considered Luke's text the primary one for the narrative of the Sinful Woman and normally kept "Mary" in John ("Mary of Bethany") distinct from both Luke's Sinful Woman and Mary Magdalene: see Ashbrook Harvey 2001a, 120–121; 2001b, 69–70; and 2006, 148–149.

καὶ στᾶσα ὀπίσω παρὰ τοὺς πόδας αὐτοῦ κλαίουσα τοῖς δάκρυσιν ἤρξατο βρέχειν τοὺς πόδας αὐτοῦ καὶ ταῖς θριξὶν τῆς κεφαλῆς αὐτῆς ἐξέμασσεν καὶ κατεφίλει τοὺς πόδας αὐτοῦ καὶ ἤλειφεν τῷ μύρῳ.

Simon thinks to himself that if Jesus were truly a prophet then he would have known that "the woman who touched him" is a sinner (οὗτος εἰ ἦν προφήτης, ἐγίνωσκεν ἂν τίς καὶ ποταπὴ ἡ γυνὴ ἥτις ἅπτεται αὐτοῦ, ὅτι ἁμαρτωλός ἐστιν). It is from this statement that the repentant woman has traditionally received the title the "Sinful Woman" among ancient Christian writers (ἡ γυνὴ ἁμαρταλός; *peccatrix*; *ḥaṭāythā*) and modern commentators (*la pécheresse*; *die Sünderin*). Recognizing Simon's doubts, Jesus tells him the parable of the two debtors. One owed 500 denarii and the other owed 50. Their creditor forgave both debts. Who then should love the creditor more? Simon responds (lit. "supposes", ὑπολαμβάνω) that the one for whom he cancelled the greater debt should love him more. Then Jesus turns to the woman and says the following to Simon:

> Do you see this woman? I entered your house; you gave me no water for my feet, but she has bathed my feet with her tears and dried them with her hair (αὕτη δὲ τοῖς δάκρυσιν ἔβρεξέν μου τοὺς πόδας καὶ ταῖς θριξὶν αὐτῆς ἐξέμαξεν). You gave me no kiss, but from the time I came in she has not stopped kissing my feet (οὐ διέλιπεν καταφιλοῦσά μου τοὺς πόδας). You did not anoint my head with oil (ἐλαίῳ), but she has anointed my feet with perfume (αὕτη δὲ μύρῳ ἤλειψεν τοὺς πόδας μου). Therefore, I tell you, her sins, which were many, have been forgiven; hence she has shown great love (ὅτι ἠγάπησεν πολύ). But the one to whom little is forgiven, loves little (Luke 7:44–47).

Luke thus turns the story of the Sinful Woman into a magisterial Christological passage, emphasizing Jesus' authority over sin and salvation, in a way unique to his narration.[4] At the same time, the intimacy expressed in the other three gospels is equally present in Luke. In fact, the focus here is even more on the woman herself than in the other versions, though Simon and those in his house—note, not the disciples—are also closely involved. The Sinful Woman story, perhaps particularly in the Lukan

---

[4] On the reception of Luke 7 as a distinctly Christological passage, see Hunt 2010.

version, comprises a narrative whole and, as such, invited sustained, imaginative exegesis among later Christian readers and writers.

II. THE SINFUL WOMAN IN THE SYRIAC TRADITION

There are three complete poems in Syriac dating to the fourth to seventh centuries which deal specifically with the Sinful Woman. The first is a *memra* spuriously attributed to Ephrem the Syrian (d. AD 373), probably originating from his students in the late fourth century.[5] The second is an anonymous dialogue poem, or *soghitha*, which consists of a dramatic dialogue between the Sinful Woman and Satan in alternating couplets, dated roughly by Sebastian Brock to the fifth to seventh centuries.[6] The third is the *memra* of Jacob of Sarug (d. 523) which is translated below. Jacob was a student of the school of Edessa, a prolific Syriac poet, and (late in life) the bishop of Batnan (Baṭnan da-Srug).[7] It should be noted that there is also an extant Greek *kontakion* on the Sinful Woman by Romanos the Melode (d. c. 555).[8] Romanos the Melode (Ῥωμανὸς ὁ Μελοδός) was a liturgical poet from Emesa (Homs) who, according to later sources, became deacon of the Church of the Theotokos in the *tou Kyrou* district of Constantinople during the reign of Anastasius I (491–518) and was a chanter in the Great Church (Hagia Sophia) under Justinian (527–565).[9] Though writing in Greek, his

---

[5] Ed. Beck 1970 1.78–91; German trans. Beck 1970, 2.99–113. For the manuscript evidence of this *memra*, see Beck 1970, 1.ix–x; as well as 1970, 2.x–xii.

[6] Ed. and trans. Brock 1988, 23–54. Another *soghitha* on the Sinful Woman edited by Brock in the same article is clearly later in date, showing the influence of Arabic poetry through its homoioteleuton (1988, 55–62).

[7] For a summary of Jacob's life and works, see now S.P. Brock s.v. "Yaʻqub of Serugh" in *GEDSH*.

[8] Ed. Grosdidier de Matons 1964–1981, 3:13–43 = SC 21; also ed. Maas and Trypanis 1963, 73–80 = Ox. 10.

[9] For the history and remains of the church *tou Kyrou* (Theotokos Kyriotissa; Kalenderhane Camii), see Striker, Kuban, and Berger 1997–2007. For further biographical details, based mainly on Byzantine Lives, see Grosdidier de Matons 1977, 178–198; Mass and Trypanis 1963, xv–xvii; and Baldwin 1991. On the relationship of Romanos to Justinian and his imperial reign, see Koder 1994 and 2008.

familiarity with Syriac poetic imagery and exegesis has been well documented.[10]

Numerous prose texts dealing exclusively or tangentially with the Sinful Woman are extant from this period, in Syriac and other Christian languages. To my knowledge there are eight surviving prose homilies specifically on the Sinful Woman: five in Syriac, two in Greek, and one in Coptic.[11] Other relevant prose texts include a Greek fragment of a homily by Origen, a Syriac prose homily "On Our Lord" by Ephrem, and a few paragraphs from the Syriac version of Ephrem's *Commentary on the Diatessaron*.[12] Ephrem's homily "On Our Lord", in particular, has such

---

[10] Paul Maas, in his magisterial article of 1910, "Das *Kontakion*," argued that Romanos relied upon Syriac poetic forms for the structure of his *kontakia* and probably for their dramatic or thematic elements as well (Maas 1910). Maas's article subsequently became the accepted word on the subject, *pace* Rodney Schork, who traced only Greek patristic influence, which, in any case, he argued was very limited (Schork 1957; 1962; cf. Maisano 2008). In more recent scholarship there is another important dissenting opinion: José Grosdidier de Matons, editor of Romanos' *kontakia* for the Sources chrétiennes series, claimed in 1977, in his otherwise definitive monograph, that Romanos was not influenced thematically by Syriac writings in the least (see also Grosdidier de Matons 1980). Following the publication of this book, however, Sebastian Brock has attempted, through a series of articles on the motif of the Binding of Isaac (Gen 22) and on other biblical themes, to reinstate Maas's view that Romanos was familiar with Syriac literature, particularly for poetic imagery and not just metrical structure (e.g. Brock 1981; 1986; 1989). Brock's (and Maas's) arguments seem to have been confirmed by subsequent work on the subject, notably that of William Petersen (e.g., 1985a; 1985b), Lucas van Rompay (1993), and Manolis Papoutsakis (2007), among others. On this debate, see further in the Appendix below.

[11] In Syriac: see Brière 1948 (text and Fr. trans.) for one homily of Severus of Antioch, Graffin 1984 (text and Fr. trans.) for three anonymous sixth-century homilies, and Sauget 1975–1976 (text and Fr. trans.) for one homily attributed to "John"; in Greek: see Field 1839, 2.436–446 (text) and Prevost 1843–1851, 3.1058–1068 (Eng. trans.) for one authentic homily of John Chrysostom on Matthew 26:6–7, and PG 59.531–536 (text and Latin trans.) for one probably pseudonymous homily of Chrysostom; in Coptic: see 'Abd Al-Masih 1958–1960 (text and Eng. trans.) for one homily also under the name of John Chrysostom.

[12] Origen: see Lienhard 1996, 173 (Eng. trans.); Ephrem, "On Our Lord": see Beck 1966 (text and Ger. trans.), and Mathews, Amar, and McVey 1994 (Eng.

specific resonances in Romanos and Jacob, that (without an intermediary text to show mutual dependence) I believe that both knew Ephrem's prose interpretation of the Sinful Woman story.[13] However, some of the texts just mentioned can be definitively placed later in composition than Jacob.[14] Nevertheless, for all of the Syriac prose texts, even a superficial glance suggests that they share a common interpretative tradition with Jacob and the Syriac poems (as well as Romanos' *kontakion*).[15]

III. JACOB OF SARUG'S *MEMRA* ON THE SINFUL WOMAN

Compared to the vast amount of scholarship on Ephrem there are relatively few studies dedicated to Jacob of Sarug.[16] Yet, he is considered by many to be the second greatest Syriac poet (e.g. Brock 1997, 37). A basic problem, of course, is that a number of Jacob's poems remain unedited, and most of those that are edited are still untranslated.[17] From 1905 to 1910, Paul Bedjan published 212 *memre* in his monumental five-volume *Homiliae Selectae Mar-Iacobi Sarugensis*, which remains today the standard edition of Jacob's poems, and which is the basis for the present edition.[18] Besides the

---

trans.); Ephrem, *Commentary on the Diatessaron*: Leloir 1963, 42–47 (text and Lat. trans.) and McCarthy 1993, 170–171 (Eng. trans.).

[13] The shared emphasis on the scene at Simon's house is particularly striking. Ashbrook Harvey 2001a, 121, draws attention to this element of the homily "On Our Lord".

[14] This is true for the three anonymous homilies in Syriac (Sauget 1975–1976) and for the homily of Pseudo-Chrysostom (PG 59.531–536), which retains part of the acrostic of Romanos' *kontakion* in its sentence structure: see Schork 1995, 20–21.

[15] Some of the Syriac prose homilies and fragments have been summarized and compared in Ashbrook Harvey 2001b and 2006, 148–155.

[16] For the bibliography on Jacob's poems, see Brock 1996, 156–160, Brock 1998, 302–303, Brock 2004, 343–344, Brock 2008, 91–92, Alwan 1986, and Brock's annual bibliographies in *Hugoye*. See also the standard encyclopedia entries: Rilliet 1994, Graffin 1974, and Tisserant 1924.

[17] See Rilliet 1993 for the early history of editions of Jacob. Brock has produced a helpful index of the incipits of the published verse homilies of Jacob, Isaac of Antioch, and Narsai (Brock 1987b).

[18] These volumes, beautifully printed in the East-Syriac script, lack a full critical apparatus and have been criticized by some for this and other reasons: see, for example, Amar 1995, 11–12. The 2006 reprint of Bedjan's edition by Gorgias Press

individual translations that continue to appear intermittently in various journals, an obscure American theological journal, *The True Vine*, has published a series of unannotated translations in English.[19] Gorgias Press's endeavor to make Jacob more widely available (and in bilingual Syriac-English editions) is thus greatly welcomed.[20]

Jacob's *memre* compose the largest part of his literary output, which includes biblical commentaries, letters, and hymns.[21] These poems are all dodecasyllabic in meter and are generally grouped into couplets according

---

includes a new sixth volume, edited by Sebastian Brock, which includes additional poems by Jacob on the Virgin Mary, a comprehensive index of incipits to Jacob's published and unpublished poems, and a detailed biography of Bedjan by Heleen van den Berg.

[19] The translations in *The True Vine* (1989–) can be found in the bibliographies cited above (n.16), along with several other translations of individual writings. Notable among the translations into English are: Kollamparampil 1997, a collection of festal homilies in prose and verse with moderate annotations (mainly biblical citations); Ashbrook Harvey 1990, a translation of Jacob's homily on Simeon the Stylite; Hansbury 1998, a selection of homilies on the Mother of God; and Amar 1995, a text and translation of Jacob's *memra* on Ephrem. The French translations include Rilliet 1986, six festal homilies in prose; Albert 1976–1977, a collection of verse homilies against the Jews; and Martin 1876, a selection of Jacob's letters. See also the edition and German translation of three homilies by Jacob on the Apostle Thomas in India by Strothmann 1976.

[20] At the time of writing, twenty percent of Jacob's homiletic corpus has been published but much more has been assigned to translators. Check the Gorgias Press website for an up-to-date listing of the volumes in the "Metrical Homilies of Mar Jacob of Sarug" series. As representative examples, see the translations by Brock 2009 (Homily on the Veil on Moses' Face), Ashbrook Harvey and Münz-Manor 2010 (Homily on Jephthah's Daughter), and McCollum 2009 (Homily on Saint Peter, When Our Lord Said, "Get Behind Me, Satan").

[21] For Jacob's writings and literary context, see Baumstark 1922, 148–158; see also Vööbus 1973–1980, 1.1–40 for a comparison of the hagiographical Lives of Jacob and a summary of his writings, grouped by form: unfortunately, Vööbus refers to the *memre* not by their incipits but by their titles, which often differ from manuscript to manuscript; see Sauget's 1974 review of Vööbus's first two volumes. Olinder 1937 is a critical edition of Jacob's letters; see also Olinder 1939; and the French translation by Graffin and Albert 2004. For the theology expressed in Jacob's writings, see Bou Mansour 1993–1999 and Kollamparampil 2010. See also the very informative collected volume of Kiraz 2010, devoted solely to Jacob.

to the sense of the verses.[22] The text of the *memra* on the Sinful Woman is comparatively short, running to only twenty-eight pages in Bedjan's edition (some run for sixty or more). Bedjan made use of five manuscripts for his edition of this poem, but the number of variants between them is relatively small, and none of the variants seriously affects the sense of the text.[23]

For the purposes of examining Jacob's *memra* on the Sinful Woman, I suggest that there are three categories into which his thematic or narrative material can be placed. The first category contains the material that only appears in Jacob's *memra* and not in the other Syriac poems or in Romanos' *kontakion*. The second category contains the material that is shared by Jacob and the Syriac verse tradition. The third category contains the material that is shared by Jacob and Romanos alone. Interestingly, there seem to be no elements that are shared by Jacob, the other Syriac poems, *and* Romanos: in particular, the perfume-seller, famous from the Ephremic *memra* and Romanos, does not appear in Jacob's poem.[24] The first category will be investigated in this section and the second and third categories in the following two sections. I have chosen to begin with the material unique to Jacob so as to demonstrate from the start what new elements Jacob has contributed to the Syriac verse tradition in his exposition of this theme. In general, the imagery from Jacob's *memra* shows a greater attention to the details of the biblical story than occurs in the other Syriac poems and also an observable tendency to interweave the different gospel versions.

In typical style, Jacob begins his *memra* with a self-reflexive section, in this case a meditation on repentance, drawing his audience into the emotions of the passage:

> For none but broken people seek your remedy;
> And for the one who has no need, not even mercy is dear to him. (13–14)

> For the one who is perfected [already], my pointless speech is a vexation,
> But for those in need, my homily—full of hope—is beautiful. (73–74)

---

[22] For the structure of his *memre*, see Blum 1983.

[23] *Memra* 51 in Bedjan 1905–1910, vol. 2, pp. 402–428; see vol. 2, pp. viii–ix, for the details of manuscripts Bedjan consulted for his edition.

[24] A fourth category, the material Romanos adopts from the Syriac poetic tradition but which does not appear in Jacob, is explored at length in a separate Appendix following the translation below.

He then narrates the basic story of Jesus' visit to the house of Simon the Pharisee, at this point following the Lukan version, which was probably the lectionary reading associated with the homily.[25] Next, the Sinful Woman is introduced by means of hunting metaphors that recur throughout the poem:

> She who was a snare for men in the places she walked
> Caught them, as if with traps, in order to corrupt them. (125–126)

> The Hunter entered and resided at the home of Simon because Simon
>   had invited him.
> And He sent and incited that dove in her nest to come to Him.[26] (153–154)

Next the theme of the fragrance is introduced, which has both olfactory and visual elements in the form of incense and smoke. While there is no mention here of the perfume-seller, the fragrance imagery is directly tied to the perfume or oil with which she anoints Jesus. This perfume becomes a major element of the imagery later in the poem when the discussion of its cost is raised among the stupefied onlookers.

> Weeping served as pure incense for her, and she brought it in with her.
> And by her groans she kindled it to make it smoke in the house of
>   atonement. (175–176)

> In the fire of her love she kindled tears like spices.
> And the fragrance (which was abundant) of her repentance grew sweet.
>   (205–206)

> The fragrance of her excellent perfume was scattered over those who
>   were reclining. <John 12:3>
> The house was exceedingly full of the pleasant smoke. <Gen. 8:21>
>   (435–436)

> It was because of the strength of its choice fragrance that they put a
>   high price on it,
> For they did not know what to say about it. (475–476)

After dwelling on the Sinful Woman's repentance and faith as a model for all Christians, Jacob begins artfully to mix the gospel narratives. He claims

---

[25] As it was for Romanos' *kontakion* (see below) and is generally today for both eastern and western lectionaries; see Ashbrook Harvey 2006, 148.

[26] See also ll. 445–446, and below.

boldly that she poured the perfume on *both* his head and his feet. The anointing of his head is from Mark and Matthew, the anointing of his feet from Luke and John. Later, the figure of Judas Iscariot is introduced, a character who appears as connected to the perfume only in John's narration of the scene.

> Treacherous Judas made use of his habitual trick, <John 12:4–6>
> He who was trying to find a way to steal the value of the oil. (477–478)

In counterpoint to the appearance of Judas, Simon the Pharisee's own heart, creatively, is now brought to the fore. These two antagonists in the *Vorlagen* (in John and Luke, respectively) are foils for the Sinful Woman's overabundant gratitude.

Like in Luke, following the actions of the Sinful Woman, Jesus tests Simon's understanding of grace. However, strikingly, right at this point, Jacob claims that Simon is also a leper, an element which comes from Mark and Matthew and which has not been mentioned previously in the homily. Up to now Jacob has only labeled Simon as "the Pharisee" (e.g. 287, 329, 391), thus sticking closely to the Lukan version. Yet now he intentionally mixes the gospel accounts:

> He cleansed the Pharisee's body from its marks,
> And he cured the prostitute's soul because she was sick. (499–500)

> He, whose manifest leprosy was cleansed, honored the Lord manifestly.
> And in his visible preparations he made a banquet. (509–510)

Jacob seems unconcerned that these are seemingly contradictory narrative elements which stem from different gospel accounts. Instead, he deftly weaves them together as a single coherent story. The change allows Jacob to close with an exhortation to the audience to be like *both* penitents, the Sinful Woman and Simon the Leper. And whereas in Luke Simon the Pharisee is painted as a true Pharisee who does not understand the egalitarian quality of grace, here he becomes, like the Sinful Woman herself, a redemptive figure. Jacob thus takes Jesus' parable very literally and points out that even though he, as the lesser debtor, is forgiven only 50, he nevertheless is still forgiven (505).

Thus, in terms of Jacob's knowledge of other poems on this scene, his most striking innovation that he makes is the greater emphasis placed on

Simon, who appears only briefly in the Ephremic *memra*.[27] Moreover, Jacob even goes so far as to compare Simon to David who was "captured by his own words" through Nathan's inquiries concerning David's adultery with Bathsheba: they both "pronounced condemnation for themselves" through their examiners, David through Nathan and Simon through Jesus (377–378; 2 Sam 11–12). Jacob criticizes Simon's doubt over Jesus' true identity and says that Simon should have recognized that Jesus was "the Son" and "the Lord of the Prophets" instead of doubting whether he was even a prophet to begin with (333–336).

Jesus' comparison between the Sinful Woman's repentance and Simon's superciliousness is part of the Lukan narrative, but the comparison is expanded here to include the gifts that each brought to Jesus. Whereas Simon presented to Jesus a "feast of bread and wine" that "comes to nothing" (401–404), the Sinful Woman offered "her prayer, her tears, her perfume, and her hair" (402). Later in the *memra*, however, the feast that Simon prepared for Jesus is, somewhat surprisingly, reckoned by Jacob as a repayment for the forgiveness that Jesus also granted to the Pharisee, a detail which is not to be found in Luke but which is connected to the cleansing of Simon's leprosy (i.e. the conflation of "Simon the Leper" from Matthew and Mark with "Simon the Pharisee" from Luke). This further solidifies Jacob's conclusion that Simon is a redemptive figure.

Unique among the Syriac poets and Romanos, Jacob includes Judas Iscariot in his *memra*. Jacob makes use of Judas' greedy comment in John 12:5 about the wasted value of the perfume, and in doing so shows further that he assumes an easy familiarity with all the gospel versions of the story:

> There was one man who set its value at 300 gold pieces and he claimed that was its worth.
>
> There was another man who said it was worth 200 and asked why it should perish.
>
> Judas had longed for its [monetary] value because he was a thief.

---

[27] Simon has a larger role in the later recension (B) of the Ephremic poem: his dialogue with a disguised Satan is contained in Appendix 1 of Beck's text (1970, 1.88–89). I can discern no elements of Simon's dialogue that show definitively that Jacob knew the later recension of the poem rather than the former: however, the theme of healing, a dominant one in Jacob's poem, does occur four times in these lines.

> He suggested a high price because he was greedy [lit. his need was excessive]. (443–446)

In Matthew it is "the disciples" who suggest that the oil was wasted (26:8); in Mark it is "some who were there" (14:4); in Luke this criticism does not occur; and in John it is "Judas Iscariot, one of his disciples (the one who was about to betray him)" (12:4). In both Mark and John the critics set the value of the oil at 300 denarii; in Matthew it is said to be worth "a large sum". None of the gospel accounts, however, include the second price that Jacob introduces here. The inclusion of Judas and the introduction of a second price are elements of the poem that show Jacob's willingness, even enthusiasm, to change the canonical versions in creative ways and his great skill at doing so.

The elements of Jacob's *memra* just discussed are not shared by any of the other Syriac poems that take up this theme, nor do they appear in Romanos. They show Jacob's imagination and poetic abilities at work. In bringing the different biblical threads together Jacob appears unconstrained by prior tradition or by the lectionary reading (likely from Luke 7). Susan Ashbrook Harvey has stated the following in connection with this poem:

> Syriac homilies and hymns [on the Sinful Woman] will follow one of two patterns: they will focus either on the episode at Simon's house following Luke 7, or the events prior to that incident as imaginatively constructed in the "Ephremic" homily, "On the Sinful Woman". (2006, 150)

This conclusion does not apply to Jacob's *memra*. While it is true that the initial setting is clearly Luke 7, by the end of the poem every gospel version has had its place in the sun, with a strong emphasis on John 12 at the end in the characters of Simon the Leper and Judas Iscariot. Moreover, classic elements of the Syriac tradition, like the perfume-seller (more below), do not appear in Jacob. In fact, the perfume-seller is one of the key elements that demonstrate the Syriac resonance of Romanos' *kontakion* on the same theme, yet Jacob does not include the least hint of him. All of this shows, as will be explained further, that tracing these thematic traditions is a complex business and the poet is liable to use the tradition in unexpected and innovative ways.

IV. Jacob and the Syriac Verse Tradition on the Sinful Woman

As expected, there are a number of parallels between Jacob and the other late antique Syriac poems on the Sinful Woman. In his edition of the *soghitha* on the Sinful Woman and Satan, Brock helpfully lists several parallels of phraseology between the *soghitha*, the homily attributed to Ephrem, and Jacob. Brock's list, however, depends first upon the word or phrase occurring in the *soghitha*, and there is evidence that Jacob appropriated material directly from the homily attributed Ephrem which the anonymous author of the *soghitha* did not.

To begin with the Syriac poems, the description of Christ as an eagle occurs in both the *soghitha* (33) and in the Ephremic *memra* (58).[28] It also occurs in Jacob's poem (423), as does the description of the Sinful Woman as a dove (154, 423), which occurs in the *soghitha* as well (32–33). Jacob uses the word ܦܚܐ "trap" or "snare" (125) to describe the Sinful Woman, just as the *soghitha* does (45), but he also uses it in other ways: for example, Jacob says that "the confused sins of an evil world are traps" and that "our Lord laid traps" to capture the Sinful Woman (5, 152, 157), the latter two being part of an elaborate "trap" conceit that extends for several lines (151–164), intersecting the imagery of the hunt which I noted above. The homily attributed to Ephrem uses the same word for "trap" when Satan contemplates how he will set a "trap" for the Sinful Woman on her way to Simon's house (234). Jacob often uses the images of both "knocking" (ܢܩܫ) on a "gate" or "door" and "opening" it as metaphors for repentance (ܠܬܪܥܐ ܐܘ ܠܬܪܥܐ) and forgiveness (ܦܬܚ ܗܘ ܬܪܥܐ), respectively (43–44; 539).[29] The image of the open door appears also in the *soghitha* (21, 57), and the Ephremic *memra*, using this same vocabulary, includes a scene in which the Sinful Woman knocks passionately on the door of Simon's house (277–278).

Most of the parallels I have just cited, which all involve imagery and language found in the *soghitha* on the Sinful Woman and Satan, are listed by Brock at the end of his edition of that *soghitha* (1988, 54). The parallels

---

[28] For eagle imagery in Syriac literature and its Middle Eastern context, see Pierre 1988, 511–516. For further references to Christ as an eagle, see Brock 1979, 14–16.

[29] Often this is the gate of his "treasury-house" (ܓܙܗ), which is opened to the one who repents (e.g. 515–516).

between the homily attributed to Ephrem and Jacob alone, however, show pointedly Jacob's knowledge and appropriation of the Ephremic text. The Ephremic *memra* has the Sinful Woman describe herself as a "bow" (ܩܫܬܐ) that "killed the good and the bad" (35). Jacob also calls the Sinful Woman a ܩܫܬܐ from whom the "accuser reigned down arrows upon onlookers" (127–128). In the same vein, the Ephremic *memra* has Satan ask himself how he will "loose arrows [ܓܐܪ̈ܐ] upon her" (236), and in Jacob's *memra* the poet himself complains that "The king of error has poured down his arrows (ܐܫܕ ܓܐܪ̈ܘܗܝ) [aiming at] my death" (9; cf. Eph 6:16). Both poets use the epithet "full of sins" (ܡܠܝܬ ܚܛܗ̈ܐ) to describe the Sinful Woman (Ephrem 307; Jacob 383) and they both call Jesus the "Sea of Mercy" (ܝܡܐ ܕܪ̈ܚܡܐ / ܝܡܐ ܕܚܢܢܐ), though they use different (but interchangeable) words for "mercy" (Ephrem 21; Jacob 4).

Probably the most striking parallel is the copious use of the verb "to weep" by both poets. The Sinful Woman is consistently described as "weeping" (ܒܟܐ) by the Ephremic *memra* (e.g. 27, 279), and Jacob has the Sinful Woman offer her weeping "as a great gift" to Jesus (93). Jacob warns that "Unless you weep [ܐܠܐ ܒܟܝܬ], He will not sympathize in your recovery," (85) and quotes Matthew 5:4, saying, "For this reason, 'Blessed are those who weep [ܛܘܒܝܗܘܢ ܠܕܒܟܝܢ],' as it is written. / One does not weep [ܐܠܐ ܐܢ ܒܟܐ] unless he has seen his wounds," (237–238). Weeping is thus for Jacob the dominant characteristic of repentance, and for both Jacob and the Ephremic *memra* the Sinful Woman is an example of true Christian contrition.[30]

These parallels between the homily attributed to Ephrem and Jacob's *memra* (and not in the *soghitha*) demonstrate that Jacob was probably well aware of the Ephremic *memra* on the Sinful Woman and tried to incorporate some of its elements, particularly its emphasis on the Sinful Woman's weeping. Most importantly, the many parallels between all three poems together show clearly that, in his exposition of this theme, Jacob stands firmly in a Syriac tradition of imagery, phraseology, and vocabulary.

---

[30] See Hunt 1998 for an in-depth examination of this theme in Ephrem; see also more generally Hunt 2004.

V. Jacob and Romanos the Melode's *Kontakion* on the Sinful Woman (SC 21; Ox. 10)

Very few scholars have attempted to explore the possibility that Romanos knew Jacob of Sarug's poetry.[31] This is partly because Jacob, as noted above, has suffered from a lack of scholarly attention, but it is also because most of the modern studies on Romanos' Syriac connections have focused on the metrical relationship of the Greek *kontakion* to the Syriac *memra* and *madrasha* poetic forms and have consequently focused on the acknowledged master of those forms, Ephrem the Syrian.[32] However, it is quite possible that Romanos knew Jacob's writings since Jacob was Romanos' elder contemporary and was the most prolific Syriac poet of the late fifth and early sixth centuries. Their lives overlapped by around thirty-five years, and, while there is no indication that they ever met, the reputation of Jacob was such that Romanos would possibly have known his work.[33]

A comparison of the two poems lends even more credence to the idea that Romanos knew Jacob's writings: on the level of "verbal agreements" or "parallels" there are certainly some strong candidates from Romanos' *kontakion* "On the Sinful Woman" (SC 21; Ox. 10).[34] The most convincing parallels, however, come from Romanos' *kontakion* "On Repentance" (SC 8; Ox. 52), which includes two paragraphs on Christ as a physician, a dominant motif in Jacob's poem but one which does not appear in the *kontakion* "On the Sinful Woman". I will explain the resonance with Romanos' poem "On Repentance" below. For the moment, let us consider four parallels between Jacob's *memra* on Sinful Woman and Romanos' *kontakion* on the same theme.

---

[31] See Brock 1981, 226–233; 1986, 66–99; and 1989, 142–143; see also Papoutsakis 2007, 38–39 n.28.

[32] E.g. Peterson 1985b.

[33] For Jacob's reputation in the sixth century and later, see Vööbus 1973–1980, 1.1–16.

[34] William Petersen claimed that his painstaking accumulation of twenty-one "verbal agreements" between Ephrem and Romanos demonstrates without doubt the "dependence" of Romanos on Ephrem. Petersen asserts that many of the "probable" or "possible" parallels found by Grosdidier de Matons, Rodney Schork, and others, "are not verbatim parallels, but allusions or the expression of similar ideas". However, there are many undefined categories in Petersen's schema: what is the precise distinction between an "agreement", a "parallel", an "echo", and an "allusion"? For further discussion of this topic, see the Appendix below.

The first parallel concerns the idea of repaying Christ for salvation. Towards the end of his *memra* Jacob says the following about both the Sinful Woman and Simon:

> The debtors even paid Him back [lit. repaid Him recompenses] for their forgiveness. (507)

Similarly, Romanos has Jesus encourage Simon to repay him in the penultimate strophe of this *kontakion*:

> ἐλθὲ οὖν πρὸς τὴν χάριν μου   ἵν' ἀποδώσῃς μοι·
> Therefore come to my grace, so that you might repay me. (21.17.8)

The fact that Romanos includes this line is interesting given that just a few lines earlier he has Jesus tell Simon the opposite:

> Οὐ δύνασαι δοῦναί μοι   ἅπερ ἐποφείλεις μοι·
> κἂν σίγησον, ἵνα σοι   χαρισθῇ ἡ ὀφειλή·
> You are not able to pay me what you owe me;
> So be quiet so that your debt might be cancelled. (21.17.1–2)

The apparently contradictory suggestion of repayment that occurs later in the strophe may be inspired by its appearance in Jacob's *memra*, for in fact this confusion over whether Christ receives any payment for his mercy is found in Jacob as well, if somewhat less pronounced:

> You do not look for a fee, Lord, so that it might be returned to you,
> For what did that prostitute give when you loved her? (31–32)

The second parallel is the common occurrence of the word for "debt-contract" in both poems. Jacob says this in the line following the one quoted above:

> They weighed out and gave (ܘܗܒܘ ܬܩܠܘ)[35] to Him [their] love instead of their debt-contracts (ܐܫܛܪܝܗܘܢ). (508)

Romanos addresses the reader in the final strophe of the *kontakion*:

> τοῦ χειρογράφου σχισθέντος,   μὴ ἄλλο ποιήσητε.
> Your debt-contract has been torn apart; do not make another. (21.18.4)

---

[35] ܐܫܛܪܝܗܘܢ comes from a variant spelling of ܫܛܪܐ: see Brockelmann 1928, 773.

The word for debt-contract in both Syriac and Greek is the same term used in Colossians 2:14, which is its only occurrence in the New Testament of both languages: "erasing the debt-contract [χειρόγραφον / ܫܛܪ ܚܘܒܐ]³⁶ that stood against us with its legal demands. He set this aside, nailing it to the cross." It is possible that both poets took this term from Colossians, but it is also possible that the allusion to this verse was suggested to Romanos by Jacob's poem, in which the Syriac word occurs at a similar place and in a similar context as the Greek word does in Romanos.³⁷

The third parallel is the inclusion of baptismal imagery by both poets. Jacob says, for example, that the "baptism of the world" is prefigured in the Sinful Woman's anointing of Jesus.

> In the oil and tears that she poured out there on the Savior,
> She prefigured the baptism of the world for the world symbolically.
> (433–434)

Jacob several times also equates the anointing of Jesus by the Sinful Woman with her own baptism (e.g. 275–276). He compares the Sinful Woman bending down to wash Jesus' feet to a catechumen descending to the baptismal font "to be purified," with the result that "the entire ritual of baptism was completed" for her as well as for the world (267–268). All of these images refer to the liturgical connection between anointing and baptism that the Syrian churches made from an early point in their history: water and oil were "inseparably linked" in the oriental celebration of the rite (Brock 1979, 23).³⁸ Interestingly, it seems that Romanos also alludes to this

---

³⁶ ܫܛܪ commonly appears in the construct form with ܚܘܒܐ ("debts") and it is likely that Jacob is playing on that typical construction by including ܚܘܒܐ ("love") in the middle of the line but not the expected ܚܘܒܐ at the end.

³⁷ It should be noted as well that this word appears in Ephrem's prose homily "On Our Lord" (44.1); while I think it is more likely that Jacob and Romanos took this word directly from the New Testament, it is also possible that both were inspired to use it by Ephrem's prose homily.

³⁸ In addition to Brock 1979, see his article on the theme of baptism in Jacob's works (1978). Traditionally, the catechumen would be anointed before and after the actual baptism, but Jacob never refers to the post-baptismal anointing in any of his writings. In this anointing the oil is not actually poured over the head but is used to mark on the forehead a sign of the cross, the ܪܘܫܡܐ, a word which often in Jacob has the pastoral connotations of the branding of sheep: see Brock 1978, 338–340.

baptismal rite in the Sinful Woman's repentant soliloquy at the beginning of his *kontakion*:

> φωτιστήριον ποιήσω   τὴν οἰκιὰν τοῦ Φαρισαίου·
> ἐκεῖ γὰρ ἀποπλύνομαι   τὰς ἁμαρτίας μου·
> ἐκεῖ καὶ καθαρίζομαι   τὰς ἀνομίας μου·
> κλαυθμῷ, ἐλαίῳ καὶ μύρῳ   κεράσω μου κολυμβήθραν
> καὶ λούομαι καὶ σμήχομαι   καὶ ἐκφεύγω
> τοῦ βορβόρου τῶν ἔργων μου.

> I shall make the Pharisee's house a baptistery.
> For there shall I cleanse my sins;
> There shall I cleanse my transgressions.
> With tears, oil, and perfume I shall mix my bath.
> And I shall be washed and cleaned and I shall be free from
> the filth of my sins. (21.6)

The appearance of the words "oil" and "perfume" in the context of baptism strongly suggests that Romanos is thinking of the Syrian rite; it also shows that he is aware of the Syriac tradition of associating the Sinful Woman with baptism and baptismal liturgy.[39]

The final parallel between the two poems is the imagery of smoke or incense that dominates the middle section of Jacob's *memra* and is present in the first and the third strophes of Romanos' *kontakion*. Jacob uses almost fifty lines in developing the image of the fragrance that arose from the oil the Sinful Woman poured out on Jesus (435–476). This is a selection of the text:

> The good perfume of the believing woman fell upon Jesus.
> The fervor and power fell also [lit. were increased] upon those who were reclining.
>
> She had stirred up the Sea of Perfumes when she approached Him.
> And excellent incense went up from Him powerfully.
>
> She anointed the Holy Christ with oil discerningly,
> And a sweet fragrance arose from Him and amazed them.

---

[39] For further thoughts on the association of the olfactory sense with Syrian liturgical elements, see Ashbrook Harvey 1998; 2001b; and 2006; for further reflections on Romanos' liturgical awareness and creativity, see Krueger 2004, 159–188; 2006; and Frank 2006.

She lit with love the Lord of the Censers lovingly.
He begat an incense so that it might also involve the apostles in the astonishment. (455–462)

In this passage the oil provides the catalyst for the aroma of Christ to overwhelm the room. Jacob goes on to suggest that Christ, the "root in an arid land" (Isa 53:2), provided the spicy power of the oil's fragrance (465–468). In a similar manner Romanos uses the image of Christ's aroma at the beginning of his *kontakion*:

Τὰ ῥήματα τοῦ Χριστοῦ   καθάπερ ἀρώματα
ῥαινόμενα πανταχοῦ   βλέπων ἡ πόρνη ποτὲ
καὶ τοῖς πιστοῖς πᾶσι   πνοὴν ζωῆς χορηγοῦντα

The prostitute then saw the words of Christ wafting everywhere like spices,
granting a breath of life to all the believers. (21.1.1–3)

Ὑπέκνισεν ἡ ὀσμὴ   τῆς τραπέζης τοῦ Χριστοῦ[40]
The scent from the table of Christ excited [the woman].[41] (21.3.1)

The similar imagery of the poems is suggestive enough of a connection, but Romanos' imaginative use of τὰ ῥήματα τοῦ Χριστοῦ in this context is not found in Jacob; if it were it would show more certainly that Romanos was appropriating this imagery from Jacob's *memra*. But, as the *kontakion* stands, it seems probable that Romanos was initially inspired by Jacob's use of the incense imagery but then appropriated it for a different thematic purpose. It should be noted, however, that the Syriac equivalent of the word ἀρώματα does occur in Jacob's poem:

---

[40] Instead of ὑπέκνισεν, Maas and Trypanis 1963, 74, print ὑπέπνευσεν, a verb which seems never to have a transitive meaning in classical or Christian literature (e.g. Acts 27:13). Moreover, there is a reasonable parallel in Jacob for ὑπέκνισεν: "He sent and incited (ܘܫܕܪ ܓܪܝ) that dove in her nest to come to Him (154)".

[41] In the second strophe the "table of Christ" is called a θυσιαστήριον, "altar" (21.2.7); this could be a reference to a number of things: the altar of the Eucharist, the altar of burnt offerings in the temple at Jerusalem (Matt 5:23; Heb 7:13; etc.), the altar of incense in the same structure (Exod 30:1, 7; Luke 1:11), the heavenly altar (Rev 6:9; 8:3; etc.), or the altar erected by Abraham to sacrifice Isaac (Gen 22:9; James 2:21).

ܗܘ̈ܝ ܩܘܢ̈ܝܗ ܕܪ̈ܝܢܐ ܗܘܘ ܒܗ ܐܘ ܐܝܢܐ ܥܩܪ̈ܐ:

What spices were crushed into it [i.e. the oil], or what roots? (449)

The common occurrence of ܩܘܢ̈ܝܐ and ἀρώματα, while not used by Jacob in the same context as Romanos, nevertheless suggests further that Romanos may have known the poem and attempted to incorporate elements from it even on a verbal level.

However, while hunting for such parallels can prove important for literary analysis, this process can only take us so far in understanding the art of the poet. "Verbal agreements" and "parallels" between two poems on the same biblical theme only tell half the literary story. To my mind, the more interesting comparisons are 1) the ways in which Jacob and Romanos *differ* in their manipulation of the same texts and 2) the ways Romanos may be appropriating imagery from Syriac, specifically from Jacob, for different purposes. I would argue that such is the case in Romanos' *kontakion* "On Repentance" (SC 8; Ox. 52).

As already noted, Romanos sticks close to the version of the Sinful Woman story in Luke and consequently has a smaller literary palette to work with. The many details that Jacob deftly interweaves from the other gospel accounts do not appear in Romanos. Although Luke 7 serves as the basic narrative framework of Jacob's poem, he has the Sinful Woman anoint *both* Jesus' head and his feet—which does not occur in any single gospel—and he includes a debate over the value of the oil, a detail that appears in every gospel *except* Luke. Further, Judas Iscariot, who appears only in the Johannine version, has a dialogue with Jesus in Jacob's poem. Thus, Romanos includes none of these extra-Lukan elements and, as I said, keeps closely to the story as it is presented in that gospel.

By contrast, very important thematic similarities exist between Jacob's *memra* on the Sinful Woman and Romanos' *kontakion* "On Repentance". The shared imagery is that of Christ as Physician, a commonly occurring motif in Syriac literature and in Romanos.[42] In an article published in 1960 titled "The Medical Motif in the *Kontakia* of Romanos the Melodist," Schork outlines the use of such imagery in Romanos but, as with his thesis on patristic resonances (1957), does not consider Syriac texts. I would like to suggest that the appearance of the "medical motif" in Romanos' poems could be a crucial factor in the debate over the influence of Syriac poetry on his *kontakia*.

---

[42] See Brock 1992, 40, and Murray 1975, 199–203.

I quote here the relevant two strophes from Romanos' *kontakion* in full:

Τὸ ἰατρεῖον τῆς μετανοίας   τοῖς γνώμῃ ἀρρωστοῦσιν ἠνέῳκται· δεῦτε,
προφθάσωμεν,   κἀκεῖθεν ῥῶσιν   ταῖς ψυχαῖς ἡμῶν λάβωμεν·
ἐν αὐτῷ γὰρ ἡ πόρνη ὑγίανεν,   ἐν αὐτῷ ἀπέθετο
καὶ ὁ Πέτρος τὴν ἄρνησιν,
ἐν αὐτῷ τὸ ἐγκάρδιον   ἄλγος Δαυὶδ ἔθραυσεν,
ἐν αὐτῷ καὶ Νινευῆται   ἰατρεύθησαν.
Μὴ οὖν ὀκνῶμεν,   ἀλλ' ἀναστῶμεν
καὶ δείξωμεν τὸ τραῦμα   τῷ Σωτῆρι,   καὶ λάβωμεν ἔμπλαστρον·
ὑπὲρ πάντα γὰρ πόθον   προσδέχεται ἡμῶν   τὴν μετάνοιαν.

Οὐκ ἀπαιτεῖται μισθὸν οὐδὲ εἷς   τῶν αὐτῷ προσελθόντων οὐδέποτε, ὅτι
οὐκ ἴσχυον   τῆς ἰατρείας   δοῦναι δῶρον ἀντάξιον·
διὰ τοῦτο δωρεὰν ὑγίαναν,   ἐκεῖνο δὲ ἔδωκαν
ὃ καὶ δοῦναι ἐδύναντο,
ἀντὶ δώρων τὰ δάκρυα·   ἔστι γὰρ καὶ φίλτατα
καὶ ἐράσμια τῷ ῥύστῃ   καὶ ποθούμενα·
μάρτυς ἡ πόρνη,   ἅμα τῷ Πέτρῳ,
Δαυὶδ καὶ Νινευῆται,   ὅτι μόνον   κλαυθμὸν προσενέγκαντες,
ὑπέπεσαν τῷ ῥύστῃ,   καὶ ἐδέξατο αὐτῶν   τὴν μετάνοιαν.
(8.1–2, ed. Grosdidier de Matons)

The infirmary of repentance has been opened to those who are sick in
    mind / purpose.
Come, let us approach and receive from it strength for our souls.
For there the Sinful Woman was made well / healed;
there Peter revoked his denial;
there David broke the strength of the pain in his heart;
there even the Ninevites were healed.
Let us not delay, but let us get up
and show our wound to the Savior and receive His salve,
since for every regret, He accepts our repentance.

Payment was never demanded of those approaching the infirmary;
since they have not the strength to anything commensurate with the gift
    of health,
accordingly, they were made well without charge.
But in return for gifts they gave the only thing they could,
their tears. For tears are cherished,
beloved, and highly treasured to the Savior.

> Witness to this are the Sinful Woman, along with Peter,
> David, and the Ninevites: offering only their weeping,
> they fell before Savior and He accepted their repentance.

The theme of weeping is dominant in Jacob's *memra*, and it appears also in this passage from Romanos as the surest sign of true repentance. In verses already quoted above, Jacob weaves the theme of tears and repentance into the incense imagery: "In the flow of her love she kindled tears like spices. / And the fragrance (which was abundant) of her repentance grew sweet" (205–206).[43] He says that the Sinful Woman's tears were the payment for her healing, just as they are in Romanos: "She gave oil and tears alone when you healed her. / Your promise wiped out a great wound with a meager payment [lit. bribe]" (33–34); and elsewhere, "She offered her tears as a fee to the Physician so that He would heal her iniquity. / He bandaged her in forgiveness, and she reached recovery" (91–92). Jacob also writes generally of the effect of tears for the penitent: "Sprinkle a drop of tears on sin when it bites you, / And believe that your wound will be eradicated, if you wish it" (81–82). The very fact that "healing" should be connected to the story of the Sinful Woman in the first place is striking, for it is really that her "debts" needed to be forgiven (according to the language of the gospels), not that her "wounds" needed to be healed.[44] The appearance of the Christ as Physician motif in both poems is a sign that Romanos possibly had Jacob's *memra* in mind when writing these two strophes, especially given that none of the biblical characters mentioned were actually in need of physical recovery.[45] Furthermore, both David and Peter (allusively) appear in Jacob's poem, the former explicitly as an example of forgiveness (375–

---

[43] He continues to develop the connection between tears and incense throughout the poem; for example: "Weeping served as pure incense for her, and she brought it in with her. / And by her groans she kindled it to make it smoke in the house of atonement." (175–176).

[44] Jacob in fact uses both metaphors for the Sinful Woman's indebtedness to Christ, but, whereas Jacob prefers the "healing" metaphor, Romanos, in his *kontakion* on the Sinful Woman prefers the "forgiving" metaphor and, as mentioned above, does not include any hint of the Christ as Physician motif.

[45] It should be remembered, however, that the Christ as Physician motif is common throughout Romanos' *kontakia*, although not as common as in Syriac literature of all periods; for other examples of this motif in Romanos, see Schork 1960.

378 and 423–424, respectively); only the "citizens of Nineveh" in Romanos are missing from the *memra*.

Other elements of Jacob's *memra* resound in the two strophes of Romanos quoted above. In Jacob, the Sinful Woman is several times described as "approaching" Christ for healing (e.g. 12), just as occurs in the first line of the Romanos passage.[46] The Sinful Woman is also described by Jacob as "uncovering her many wounds" and "exposing her soul" to the "Physician" and the "Great Flood of holiness" (251; 281). The idea of a "fee" being offered to Christ in return for health occurs in a number of passages in Jacob (91; 18; 31).[47] All of these parallels suggest strongly, to my mind, that Romanos was either influenced by Jacob's *memra* in composing the first two stanzas of his *kontakion* "On Repentance" or they shared a mutual source for such material.

While it may be somewhat surprising that such likely parallels between Jacob and Romanos do not appear in the *kontakion* on the Sinful Woman, it can serve as a reminder that Romanos was a literary artist and perfectly able to draw inspiration and to appropriate material from a variety of poems. Jacob, too, shows himself to be a literary artist in the way he interweaves all four gospel narratives into his poem. Romanos does not do this, but draws deeply on the Syriac interpretative tradition, even while steering a strict course inside the bounds of the given lection. Thus both authors, roughly contemporary with one another in the sixth-century East, approach the Sinful Woman in different yet complimentary ways.

VI. Conclusion

An examination of Jacob of Sarug's *memra* on the Sinful Woman within the Syriac verse tradition on this theme shows that Jacob probably knew the Ephremic *memra* and that, in his exposition of the motif as well as in his vocabulary and phrasing, he stands firmly within the Syriac tradition as typified by the *soghitha* on the Sinful Woman and Satan. A comparison of Jacob's *memra* to Romanos' *kontakion* on the Sinful Woman shows that Romanos possibly knew and appropriated material from Jacob. More important, however, for the overall issue of Romanos' acquaintance with and appropriation of Syriac poetry is the appearance of a shared, central

---

[46] Other "approach" passages in Jacob include ll. 256, 257, 264, 417 (quoting Luke 7:39), 425, and 457.

[47] This idea also appears in Ephrem's prose homily "On Our Lord" (44.1).

element of Jacob's *memra* on the Sinful Woman in Romanos' *kontakion* on repentance. The dominance of weeping imagery in the *memra* suggests that Romanos appropriated it from Jacob, and Romanos' inclusion of David and Peter, as well as the ancillary theme of tears as the physician's fee, makes this connection more probable. However, the significance of this connection lies not in the verbal borrowings per se, but in Romanos' creative use of material from the corpus of Syriac poetry in narrative contexts that it did not originally appear in. While this conclusion may make the job of the allusion-hunter much more difficult, it nevertheless testifies to the exciting possibilities of artistic freedom in the sixth century, across linguistic and theological lines.

It is my hope that more studies will be made on the interconnections of Jacob's poems with the liturgical poetry of Late Antiquity, in both Syriac and Greek. Even if scholars of the future reach the conclusion that Romanos' direct knowledge of Jacob's poetry is on the whole minimal, the many similarities in their independent modes of exposition are nevertheless striking and should be appreciated for what they say about the arsenal of imagery, characters, and language shared among eastern liturgical poets during this period. Jacob's *memra* and Romanos' *kontakion* on the Sinful Woman are just two examples of this parallel creative expression that depended on a close reading of the scriptures and a willingness to expand—and sometimes to combine and willfully reimagine—the familiar stories from the gospels in order to produce new and vivid narratives for their audiences.

TEXT AND TRANSLATION

JACOB OF SARUG'S HOMILY ON THE SINFUL WOMAN [ED. BEDJAN 1905–1910, 2.402–428]

MEMRA 51 OF HOLY MAR JACOB, "ON THE SINFUL WOMAN WHOSE SINS OUR LORD FORGAVE (MARY MAGDALENE)"

Jacob's Prayer of Repentance

{402} Lord, I long for your forgiveness to come to me.   1
Give me tears that I may ask for mercy while there is still time.

I thirst for mercy and without it I cannot exist.
Sea of Mercy, pour out on me the streams of your kindness.

The confused sins of an evil world are traps for me.   5
By your mercy, Lord, destroy them, and I will escape.

Like a legion thirsting for blood my sins surround me.
Come, Mighty Warrior, to the aid of a humble worker.

The King of Error has poured down his arrows [aiming at] my death. <Eph 6:16>
Commander, apply to me your remedy by which I may be healed.   10

Your treasury is not too small to give mercy to those who do not deserve it:
Because even when a prostitute approached you, you loved her deeply.

B 51

402

For none but broken people seek your remedy;
And for the one who has no need, not even mercy is dear to him.

{403} The good physician, however, only excels in ulcers. 15
For what does he add to the sound body if it should approach him?

It is in wounds that he shows the power of his skill.
Justly does he receive a fee and a reputation according to his ability to heal.

The physician shines on the stricken ones when they are healed,
And Your great compassion [shines] on sinners when they are absolved. 20

Because you have mercy, I acquired sins, and thus I expect
That whenever you pardon me, your compassion will shine in me.

I do not say that my transgression is too great to forgive, <Gen 4:13>
Because your compassion is even greater than the sea: purify me in it!

I prepared the work for your mercy every day when I was a sinner, 25
So you should not be idle from forgiveness, because it is dear to you.

For the physician wishes that the ulcers may increase in his neighborhood,
So that he might acquire from them both profits and praises.

Here are some wounds: bring your medication that it might shine on me,
Because it is very beautiful to you when you heal the stricken ones. 30

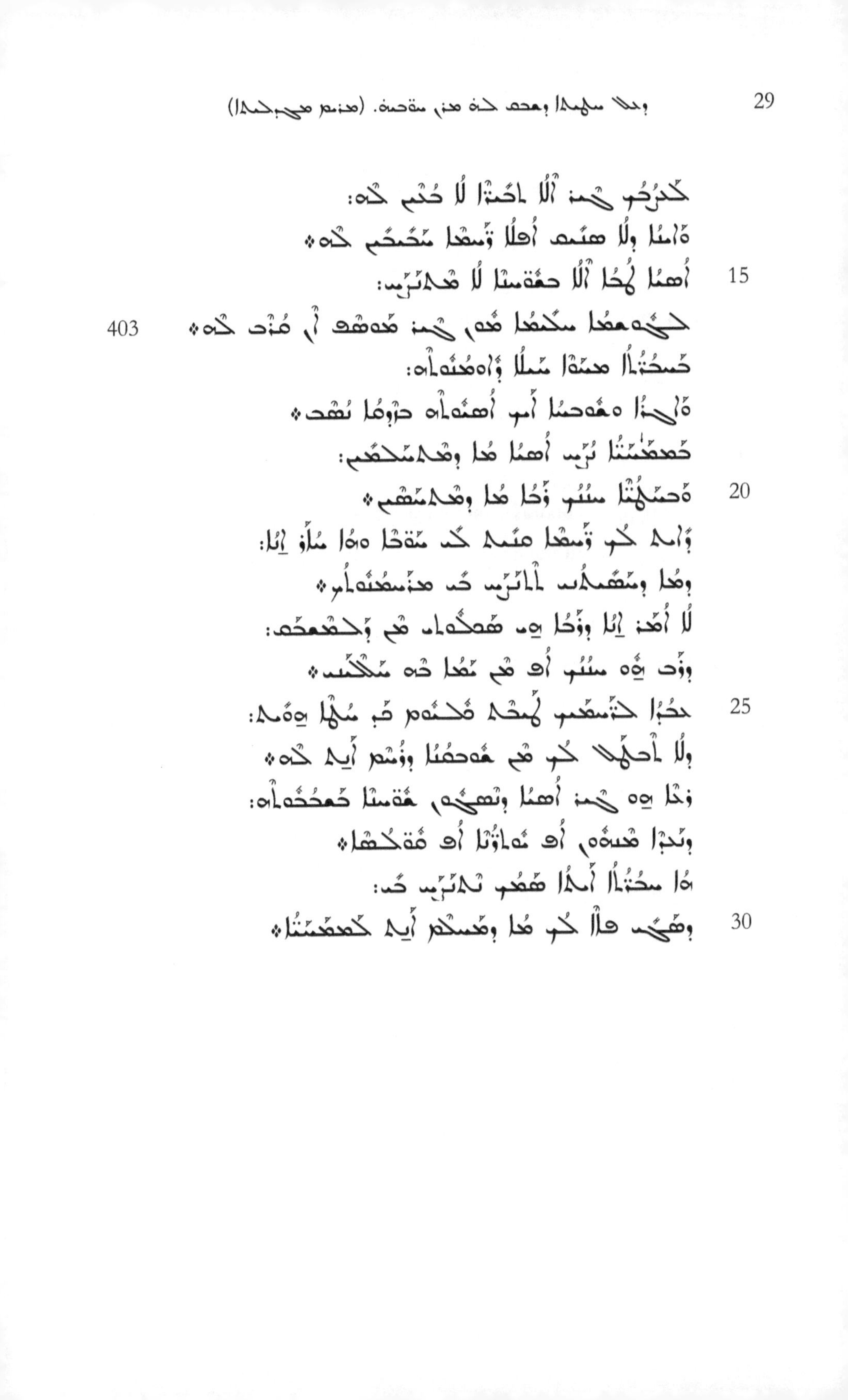

You do not look for a fee, Lord, so that it might be returned to you,
For what did that prostitute give when you loved her?

She gave oil and tears alone when you healed her.[1]
Your promise wiped out a great wound with a meager payment [lit. bribe].[2]

The river of fire that was threatening the defiled woman,   35
In a drop of tears that she sprinkled on it, she quenched it.

{404}   The negligible water that the eyes [of this woman], full of impurities, poured forth
Fell upon the flood of flame and stopped it.

Heed the Example of the Sinful Woman

I will speak of her whose story is loved by members of her rank,
For when they listen it will sprinkle hope on their infirmities.   40

The homily is received by the penitent, who will heed it,
For they also thirst for forgiveness just as she did.

Let no one abandon the great door of repentance,
Because even the prostitute, when she knocked on it, received salvation.

Let whoever sins not come close to losing hope,   45
But let him be bold like the prostitute, and then he will be pardoned.

---

[1] This is the first mention of a theme that will recur throughout the poem: the mixture of water and oil, symbolizing death and resurrection through the sacrament of baptism.

[2] Jacob is engaging in some characteristic alliteration here: the Syriac words for "wound" and "bribe" differ by only one letter.

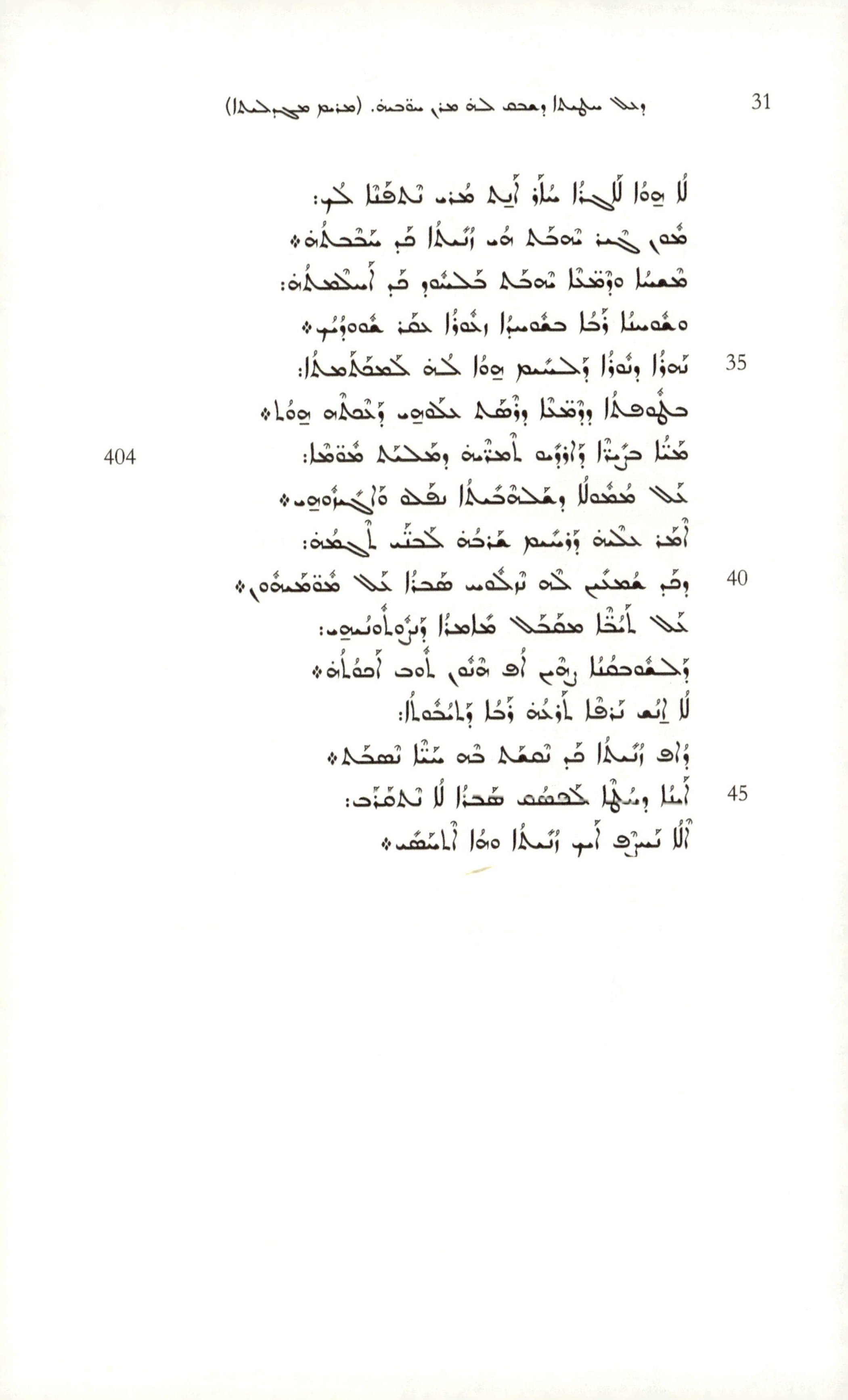

لَا :

Whoever repents, if he sins again, he should once more make supplication,
For there is no limit or special time for repentance.

If he is soiled ten thousand times, he can be purified
And however often he falls, he can stand up again if he tries hard.   50

If one sins and returns to supplicate, then he will be received,
Because there is not a time when the door to repentance is closed.

Even if my brother goes astray seventy-seven times, I will forgive him.
How much more will the Merciful One forgive the one who seeks Him?

Do not be wearied by making a petition [for mercy], no matter how much you have sinned.   55
It does not weary the Compassionate One when He forgives you.

Even if you do not have pity on your body, increasing its ulcers,
It is easy for the physician to heal you, however often you seek him.

{405}   And [even if] you do not hate that you increase the wounds on your body,
Your Physician is skilled and will shine out in your recovery.   60

If it is pleasing to you, every day you may be both a destroyer and a builder.
It does not weary Him to receive your labor, however much you seek Him.

Even if you know that time is left to you before the end,
Do not doubt your forgiveness, if you repent.

Even if the time of your death were not a secret from you,   65
Atonement is not far from you, if you repent.

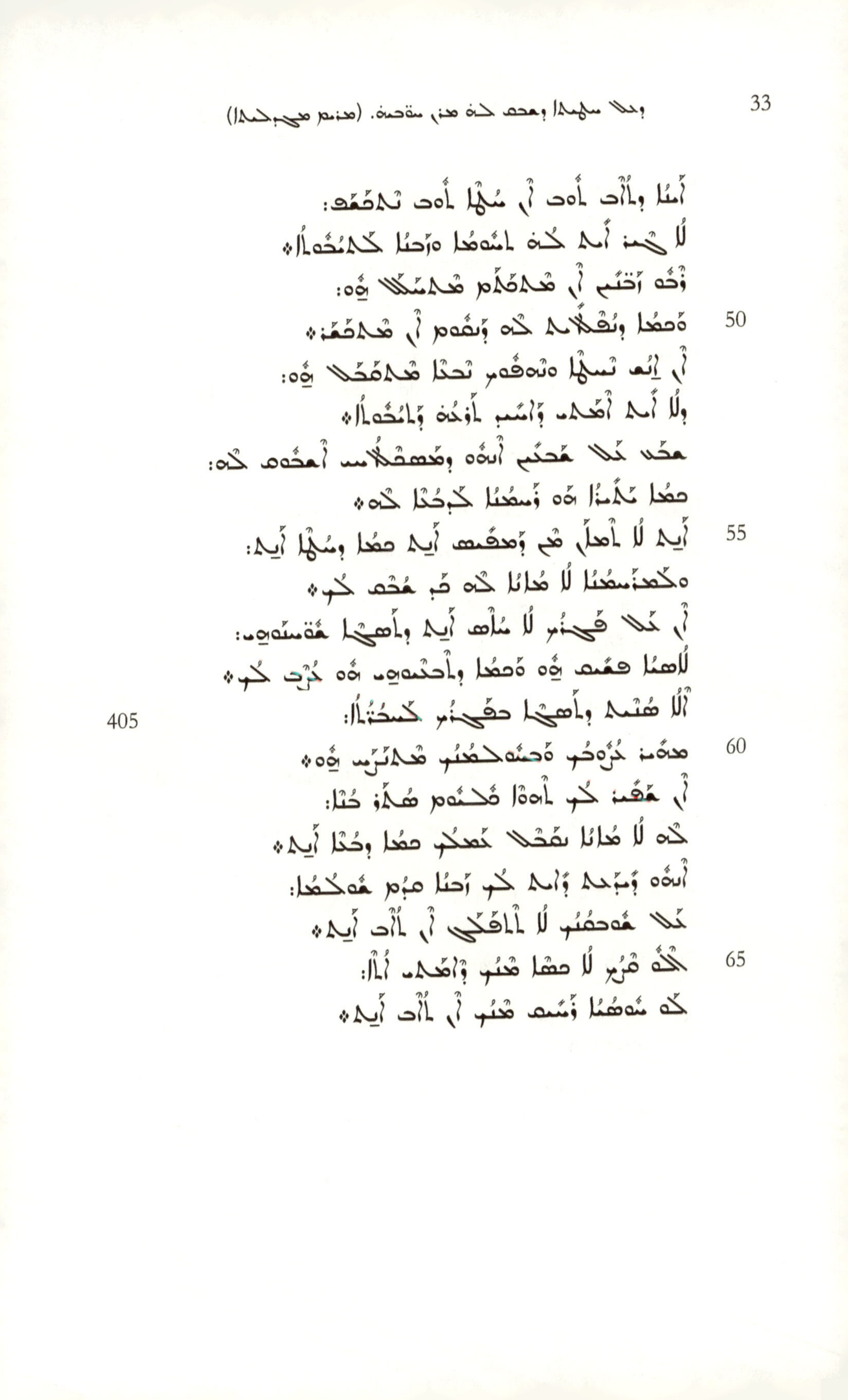

405

If you repent seventy-seven times in one day,
They will not shut the door in your face once you knock.

If a sin wounds you at night on your bed,
Go to the Physician's house in the morning, and He will cure you.   70

If you discover another ulcer by daylight,
Tread on the Physician's threshold in the evening, and He will heal you.

For the one who is perfected [already], my pointless speech is a vexation,
But for those in need, my homily—full of hope—is beautiful.

The Lord of the House is good for His part to the one who seeks Him,   75
[For] even if your eye is evil, He will not harm it. <Matt 5:29>

Or does He not have authority over His treasury-house since it is His,
To make rich from it, without hindrance, everyone who is in need?

Ask, sinful one, because He who takes pity on everyone is good in His part.

{406} However much you seek Him, He will yield, for He is not wearied.   80

Sprinkle a drop of tears on sin when it bites you,
And believe that your wound will be eradicated, if you wish it.

Gush forth a river of tears against iniquity, and the river will stifle it.
Let weeping enshroud it just like a dead man, and you will escape from it.

Unless you weep, you will not feel pain in your recovery.   85
There will not even be a need for a Physician to bandage your wounds.

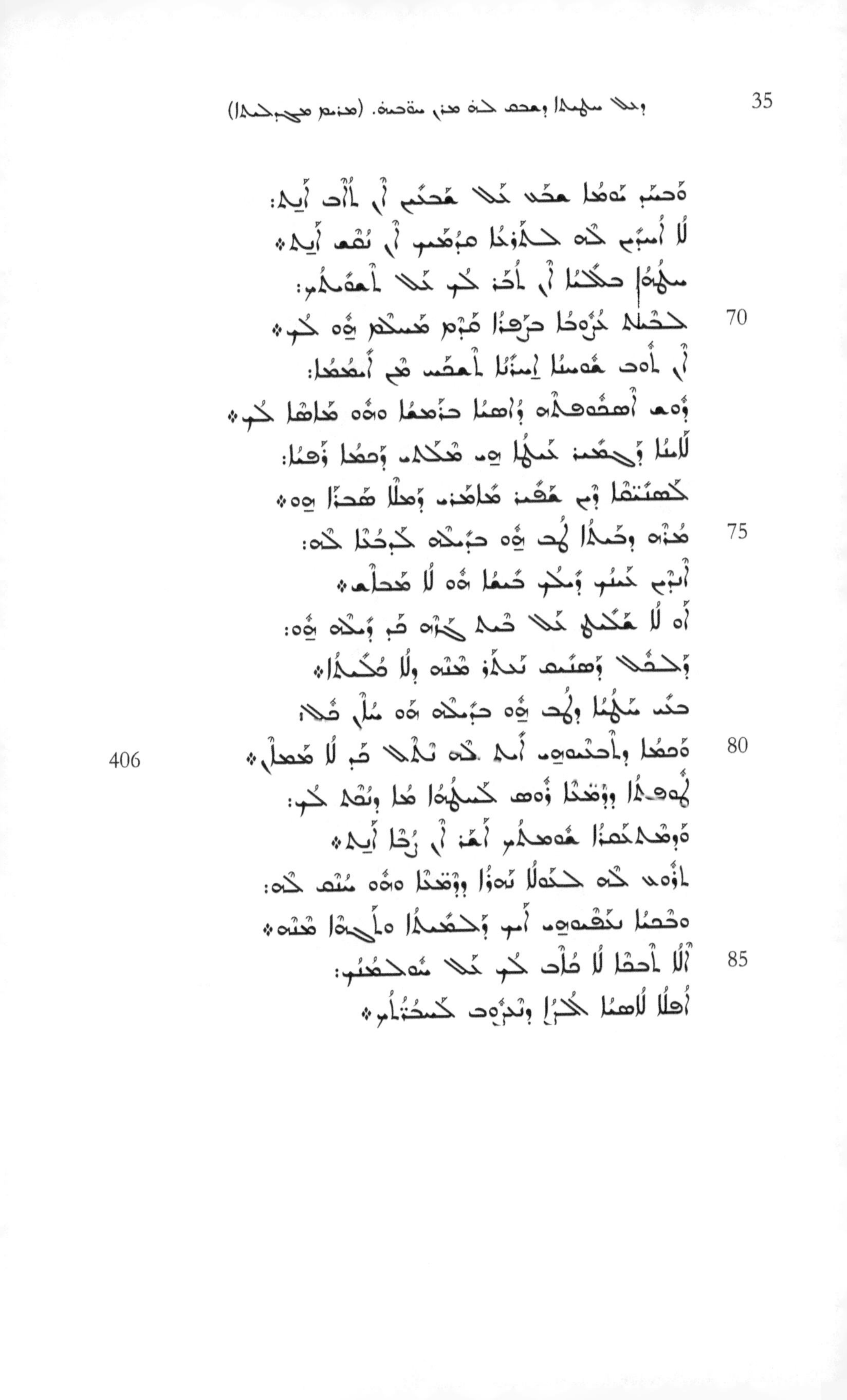

Has habit led you to come and pray, but you fail to receive?
It is because only by [true] suffering are the ulcers of iniquity healed.

Even the prostitute really wept when she was healed.
For the pain of iniquity was swelling in her, [wanting] to leave.   90

She offered her tears as a fee to the Physician so that He would heal her iniquity.
He bandaged her in forgiveness, and she reached recovery.

She bore her weeping as a great gift and entered His presence;
He greatly increased her honor, both in forgiveness and in reputation.

Tears stand as a token of love when they are seen,   95
And for this reason they are loved by Him who made atonement for all.

The body is loved when it is stricken with wounds.
It moves the eye to weep for its beloved.

For the Merciful One seeks for love to be presented to Him.
He does not take a gift from anyone when He heals him.   100

{407}   He runs to a good intention to love it.
For it takes the place of sacrifice and libation. <Hos 6:6; Matt 9:13>

It was not to judge the world that He came when He was sent. <John 3:17; 8:15>
He devised a way to vivify the world because He is full of mercy.

He was conversing with the sinners and prostitutes,   105
For the Physician is useful to these, to bandage them. <Matt 9:12>

In order to remit sins, our Lord set His path in the world.
And He was loving everyone who needed forgiveness.

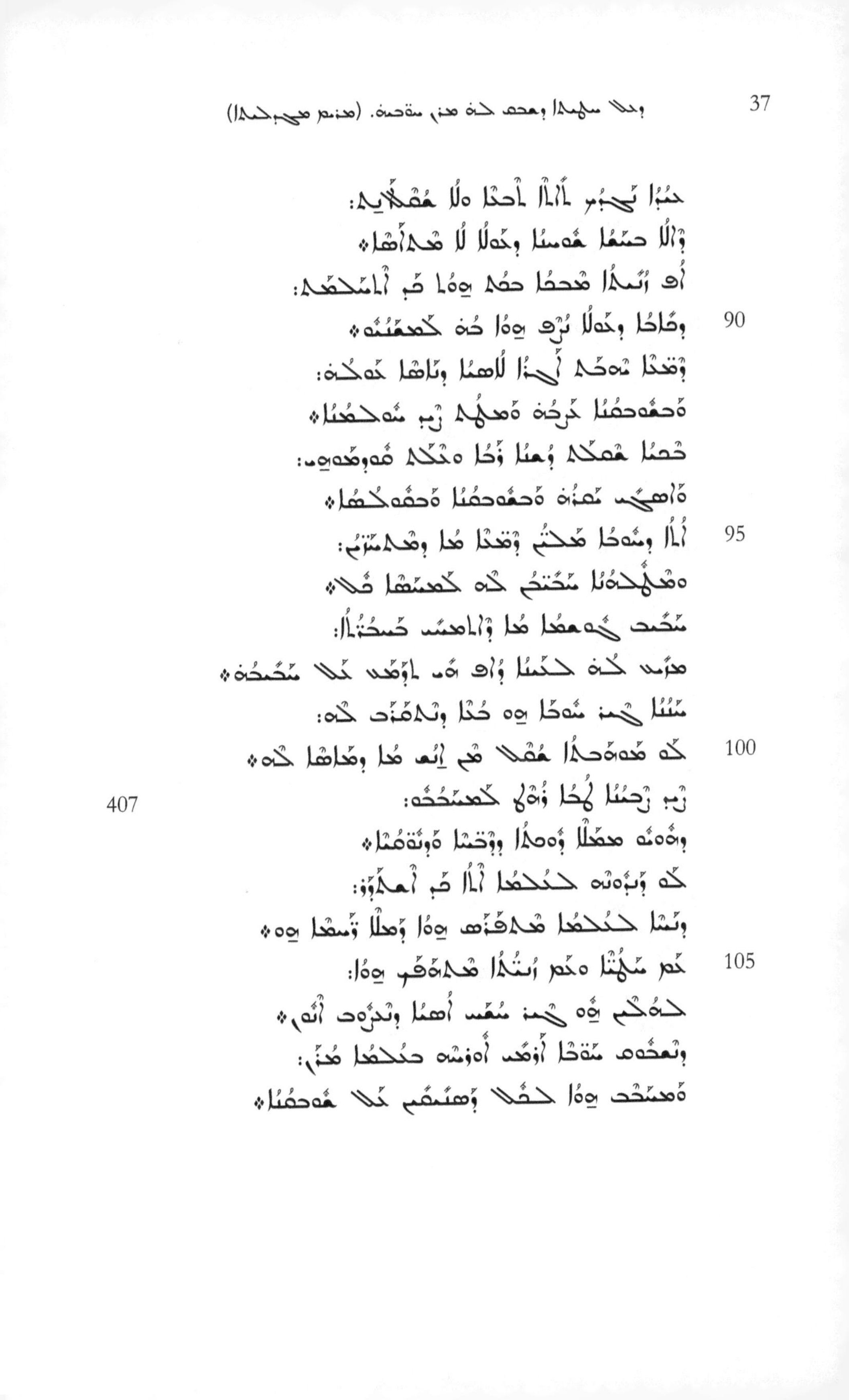

He came from His place to take the iniquity of the whole world.
And in [our] wounds He shows the strength of His sweetness.
110

The Lord Seeks Sinners

The Feeder of Families had been invited to Simon's house. <Luke 7:36; Matt 26:6; Mark 14:3>
His love led Him down to be a wayfarer, just as He was invited.

He was affable and (although pure) mixed [with sinners]; He was peaceful and full of mercy.
He was everything with everyone so that He might gain everyone wisely. <1 Cor 9:22; 10:33>

If they invited Him to the tax-collector's house, then He would mix [with them]. <Matt 9:9–13; Mark 2:13–17; Luke 5:27–32; 19:1–10>
115
And if the Pharisees called Him, again He would go. <Luke 11:37–54>

They sought bread, and He multiplied it in the desert without a baker. <Matt 14:13–21; Mark 6:30–44; 8:1–10; John 6:1–13>
They invited Him to eat, and He went along with them, just as a neighbor would.

Those who were in need sought recovery and received it from Him.
They sought atonement and He, as the Good One, offered it to all who asked Him.
120

The seekers took everything they asked for from His treasury house,
{408} So on every side He was full of mercy to those who asked Him.

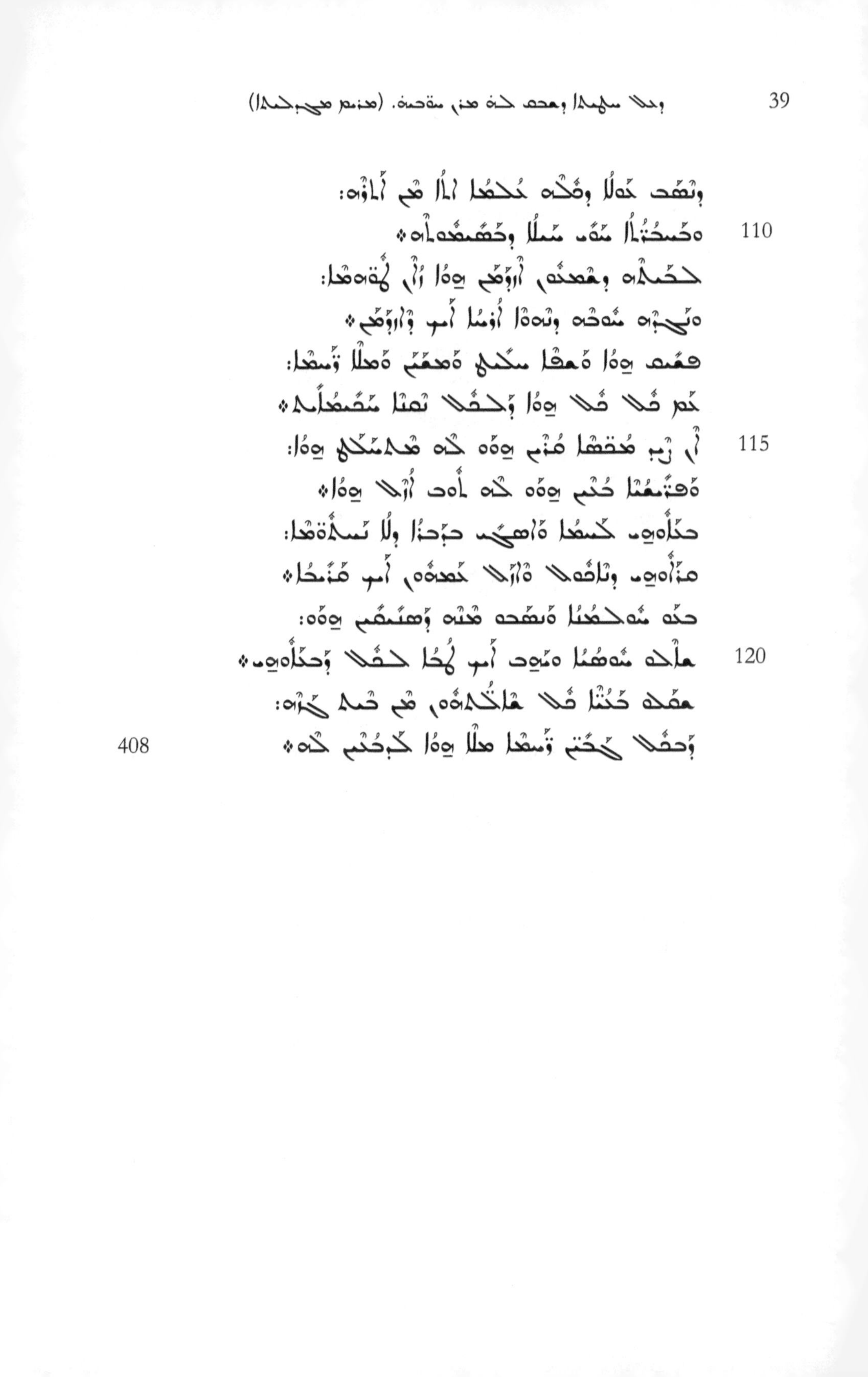

Simon invited [Jesus] and He went with [Simon] to supper.
The Sinful Woman sought out forgiveness for her sins and took it from Him.

She who was a snare for men in the places she walked   125
Caught them, as if with traps, in order to corrupt them.

She who was a choice bow for the Accuser,
From her he rained down arrows of desire upon onlookers.

She who took men captive through her lustful beauty,
After her young men wandered from their normal lives, as into   130
a pathless desert.

She who hated the pure path of sexual intercourse
In her prostitution wickedly destroyed the law.

She who wasted many of her days in depravity
With liars acted immorally in her corruption.

She who ambushed [men] on the streets like a brigand   135
Caught the merchants with her beauty in order to crush them.

She who made a division between husbands and their wives
In such conflicts took away the life of the spouses.

She who labored in prostitution from her youth
Established a festival for adultery in a place and polluted it.   140

She to whom seven demons (lovers of adultery) adhered <Matt 12:43–45; Luke 11:24–25>
Through them hunted young men to make them fornicate with her.

{409}   She who was an abode of iniquity, which would be celebrated in it,
Falsehood dwelt within her, and it had rebelled against justice.

She who despised both noble living and chastity,   145
Behaved lustfully in her actions.

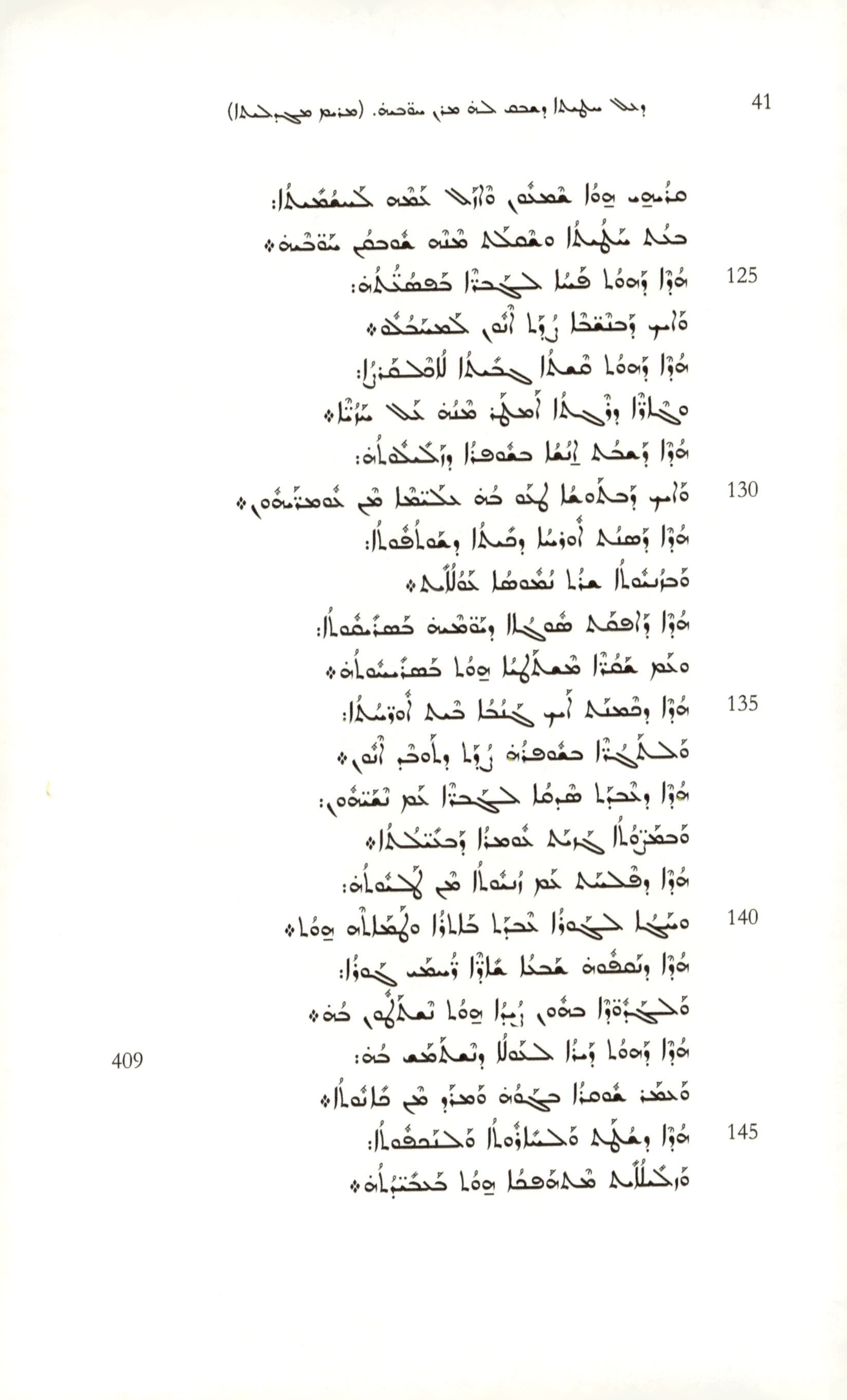

She whom the Evil One set in Judah as a target for iniquity,
The lovers of adultery were aiming at her in their affairs.

She who loved vanity along with the emptiness of prostitution
Hated pure marriage which ought to have been honored by her. 150

It was for her, the vain woman in her acts and deeds,
That our Lord laid a trap of mercy to capture her.

The Hunter entered and resided at the home of Simon because Simon had invited Him.
And He sent and incited that dove in her nest to come to Him.

Mercy went away to hunt down the rebellious woman, 155
Who had fled from the cultivated land to the great desert.

The Hunter ran and set traps in the streets [which she frequented].
He bound her with love so that she might not wander in vain.

He was spreading out a great net of repentance before her.
And she slithered and entered its great womb in naïveté. 160

The message of salvation was bait for the wild woman.
And when she was engrossed in it, she came into the net of the House of God.

The news of Jesus was spread out in front of her, and it excited her.

{410}

And when she was pasturing in it she was captivated by it to be [made] His.

She learned in her diligence that our Lord was forgiving sins; 165
Since she was needing forgiveness, she ran to His appointed place.

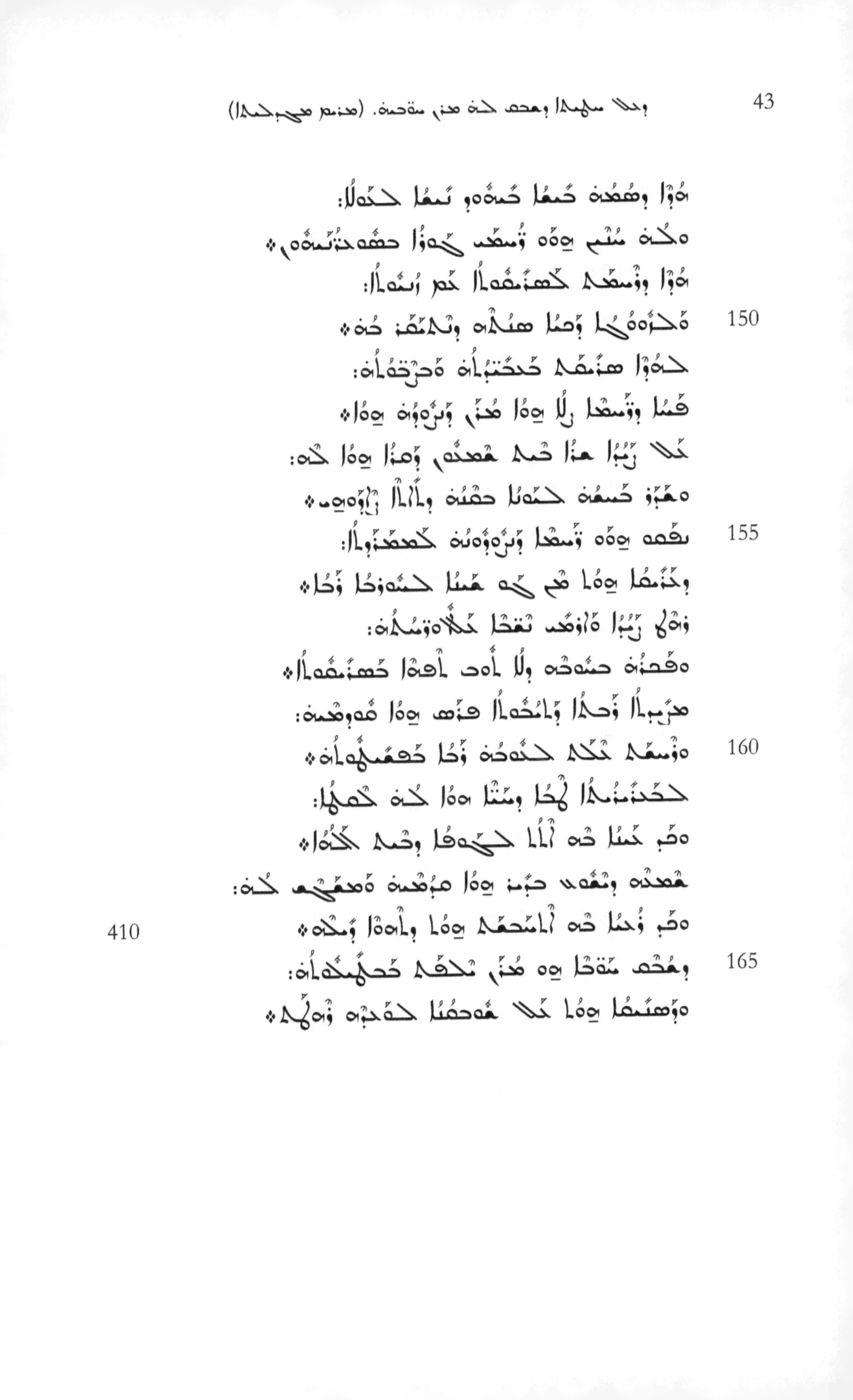

Iniquity lay in ambush in the form of a Lion, [ready] to crush her, <1 Pet 5:8>
But she ran to Jesus the Physician so that He might devise [a remedy] for her.

Her sins afflicted her with a multitude of wounds.
And she sought healing from the greatest of all physicians.   170

The sagacious woman took with her a choice oil;
She arrived at Simon's house and entered the presence of our Savior.

She was not ashamed in front of the many people reclining there,
For no one is ashamed before the doctor to confess his ulcer.

Weeping served as pure incense for her, and she brought it in with her.   175
And by her groans she kindled it to make it smoke in the house of atonement.

She was a priest for herself who would advocate forgiveness.
She offered her will with feeling for reconciliation.

She, the mistress of sins, stood behind Jesus, <Luke 7:38>
And she made a petition in sighs to offer to Him.   180

The Sinful Woman Asks for Healing

Such words as these were spoken by the prostitute
When she was praying to the Forgiver of Sins, that He might be reconciled to her:

"Lord, I know that mercy sent you to come to the land.
It directed your path to sinners, that you might show pity.

Show your strength to me, a wretched woman, because I need it;   185

{411} And so that the world, which needs redemption, might be instructed through me.

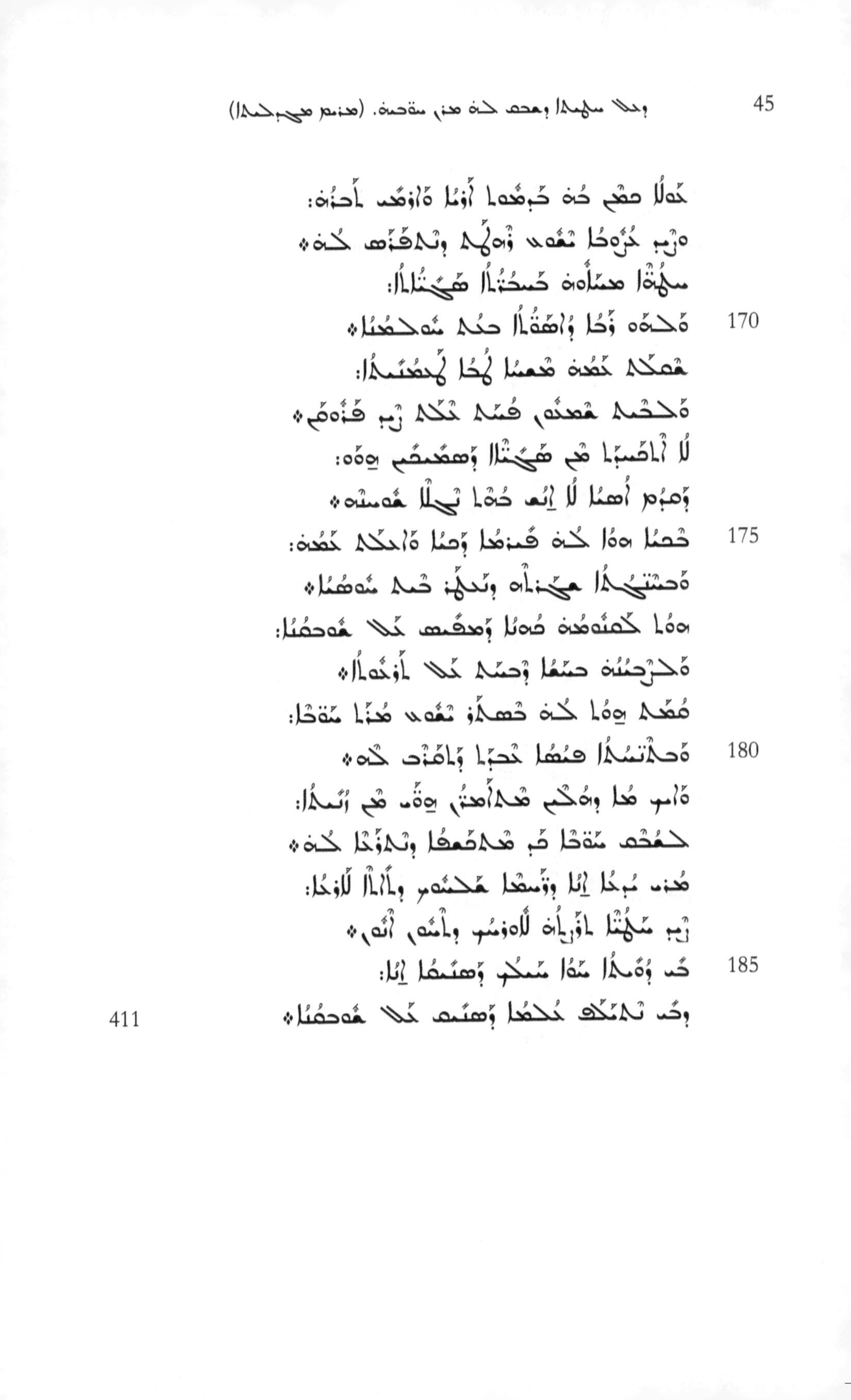

The ulcer of iniquity destroyed me every day and increased my pain.
Good Physician, bandage the sick woman who petitions you.

The evil one buried traps for me and caught me with his cunning.
Hunter of Truth, crush them, and I will be yours. 190

The winter of sins stripped bare my beautiful branches.
Lord, make blessed hope blossom in you just as in Nisan.

Into the clear soul which the demons that adhered to it muddied,
Enter, Strong One, and expel them so that I might escape. <cf. Mark 3:27>

I have been a field of thorns in my sins for quite a long time now. <Mark 4:7; Matt 13:7; Luke 8:7> 195
Plowman of Truth, weed out the bitter things from your field.

The accuser bound me to his yoke to collaborate with him.
Lord of Truth, give me freedom, for I am looking to you.

A robber beat me and then drew me into a scandalous life [that lasted] for a long time.
Great Savior, bring me into your fortress so that I might be sheltered by it. 200

The world is an ocean that in its swells took me to kill me.
Haven of Life, let me be drawn in by you from the storms."

Words of passion were born from the penitent woman.
And mercy was poured out by the Merciful One for [her] forgiveness.

In the fire of her love she kindled tears like spices. 205
And the fragrance (which was abundant) of her repentance grew sweet.

{412} Our Lord was to her like a mirror and she looked into it.
She saw herself, that she was stricken with wounds.

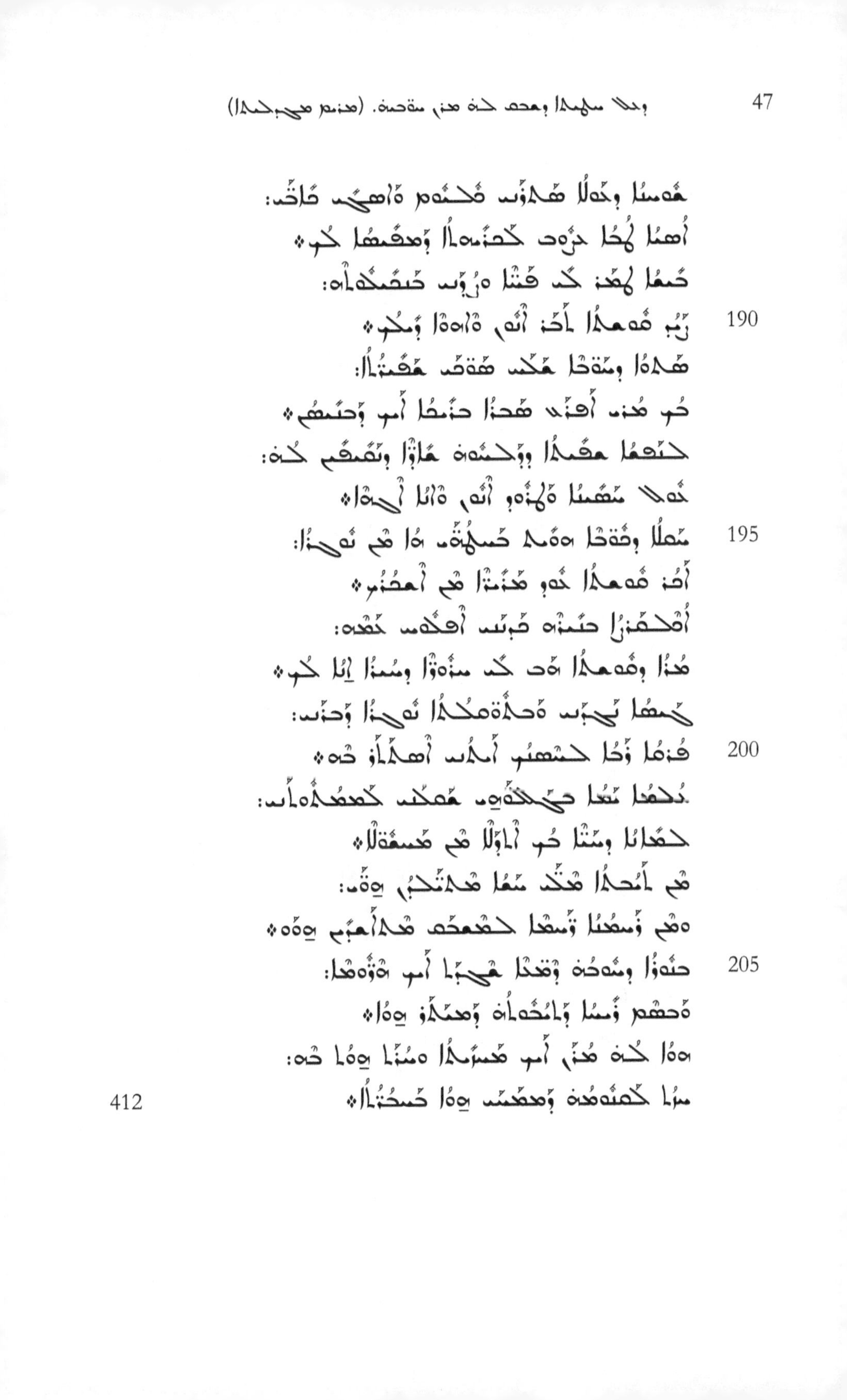

It was dark when she drew near to the Luminary,
And as she saw herself terror seized her because of how ugly   210
she was.

The Soul in Darkness

When someone sins he really forgets what he does,
And in the darkness of error he commits iniquity, although he is unaware of it.

Sin enters and blinds the soul and perturbs it.
[The soul] does not see that there is an odious mark which is cultivated in it.

If the soul had not really been following after iniquity,   215
The sin in the soul would not have been committed because [the soul] is refined.

[The soul] hates to commit sin, but in error opportunities [to sin] enter.
[Error] perturbs the soul, then [the soul] errs and is seduced.

The Evil One enters and covers [the soul] with his cunning.
Then sin hands [the soul] over to darkness so that it might cleave to [sin].   220

[Sin] places upon [the soul's] transparency the filth of its bitterness.
And when [the soul] is perturbed then it sins unwittingly.

A cloud of iniquity covers [the soul's] face when sin belongs to it.
And [the soul] wanders in darkness and does not understand what it has done.

But when the light from grace reaches the soul,   225
It is startled so that it will leave the stumbling-blocks through which it was erring.

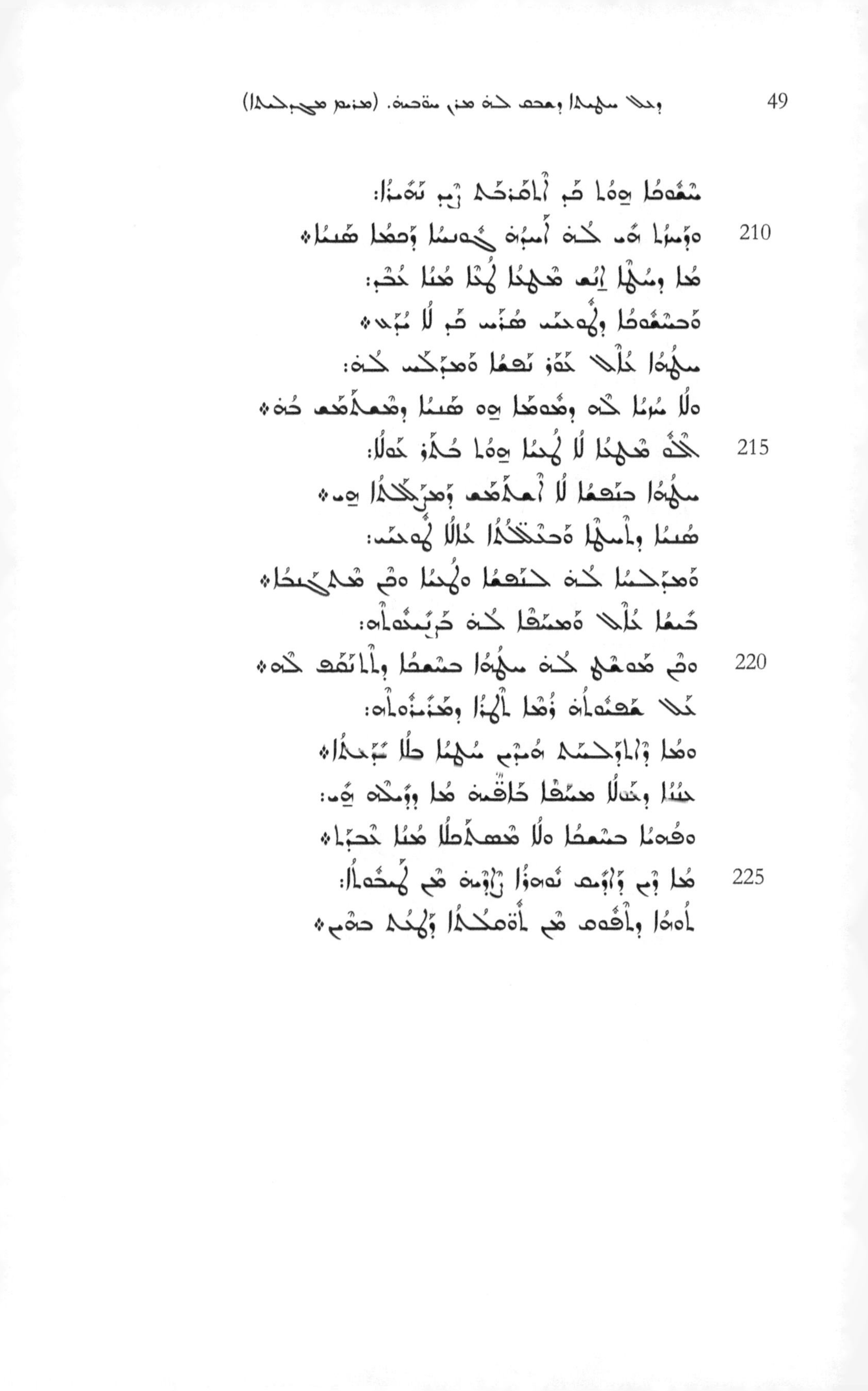

It sees the iniquity and understands that [iniquity] is an odious blemish.
And it flees from it when it finds shelter in repentance.

{413} [The Sinful Woman's soul] was astonished at how deep it had sunk when it was seduced.
And it calls out diligently in pain that it might return to its own.   230

And the soul is enlightened when it draws near to repentance.
And it runs to attain its former beauty which had been corrupted.

Contrition and tears fall from it after it recollected
The kind of spots that iniquity made on it when it drew near to [iniquity].

All kinds of bitter groans were born inside it,   235
For it saw the ulcers of iniquity that had multiplied in it.

For this reason, "Blessed are those who weep," as it is written! <Matt 5:4>
One does not weep unless he has seen his wounds.

The Prostitute's Rebirth

The prostitute wept because she saw that her wounds were many.
Her soul understood, and terror seized her because of her corruption.   240

Jesus the Sun rose and gave her light powerfully,
And He showed her that her path was blocked by offences.

"Light had shined in the darkness" over the wretched girl, <John 1:5>
And she took hold of His feet and repented to Him lovingly.

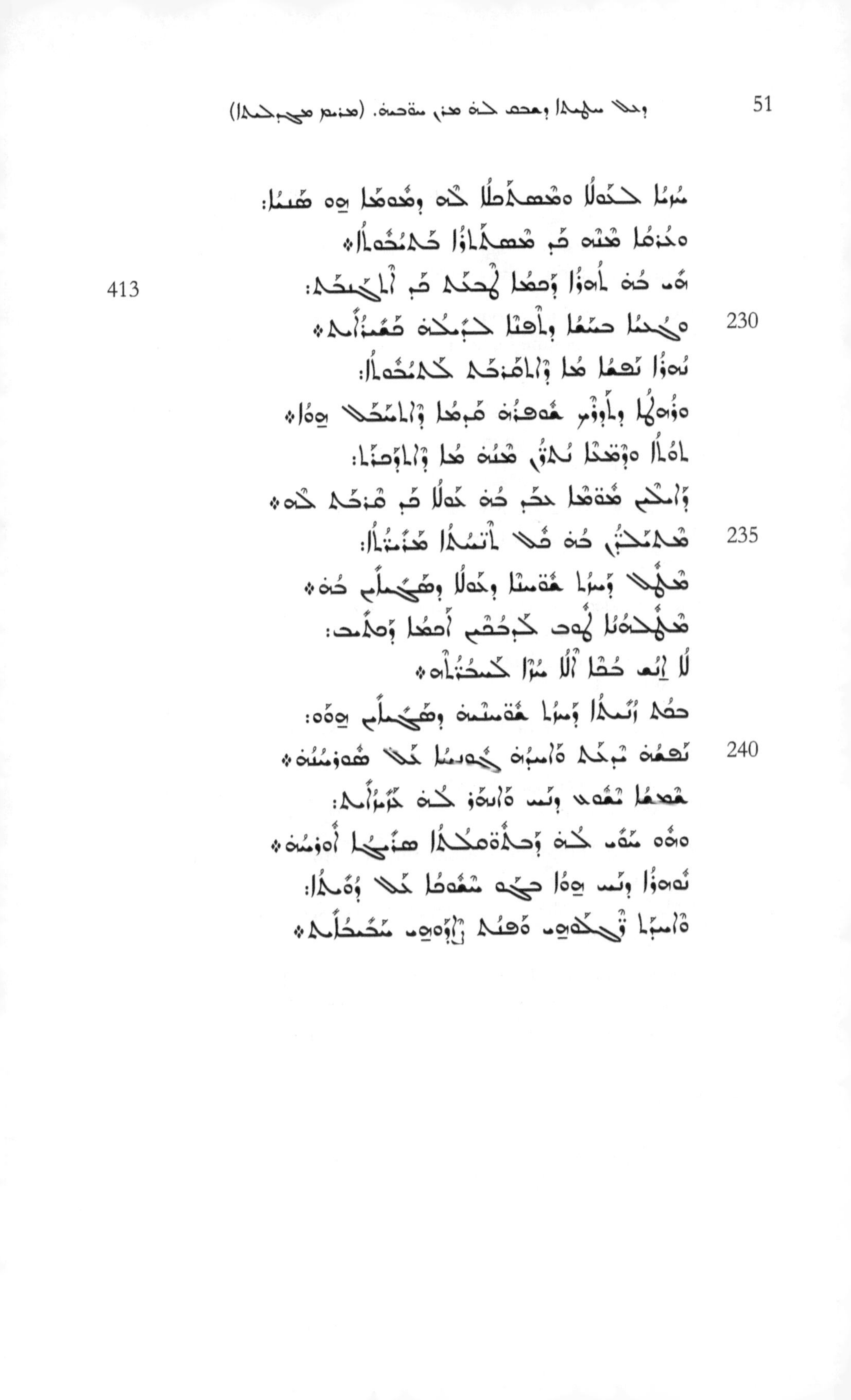

The radiance of the Father shined and gave light to the woman who was darkened, 245
And in the beams of light she drew near to Him so that she might be purified through Him.

[Her] soul saw the glorious image of the Great Light,
And it took from the Light brightness so that it might flee from darkness.

{414} She saw herself corrupted by odious iniquity,
And she shed tears upon the Physician so that He might heal her wounds. 250

She uncovered her many wounds to bring them near to Him,
And she shed tears with passion to show that it was bitter to her.

She sprinkled the Physician with excellent perfume when He was healing her,
So that everyone might see a token of her love in the fragrance of the oil.

She poured this oil on both His head and His feet, <Matt 26:7; Mark 14:3; Luke 7:38; John 12:3> 255
Because on every side He was full of mercy to the one who approaches Him.

He offered Himself to the one full of blemishes to approach Him,
And, just as she had sought to do, she caressed Him discerningly.

She took hold of His head, and He did not forbid this defiled woman from doing so. <Mark 14:3; Matt 26:7>
She grasped His feet, and He let her do as she wished. <Luke 7:38; John 12:3> 260

She sprinkled Him with tears, and He did not draw back from the wretched girl.
She kissed Him with passion, and, although she was a prostitute, He did not drive her away.

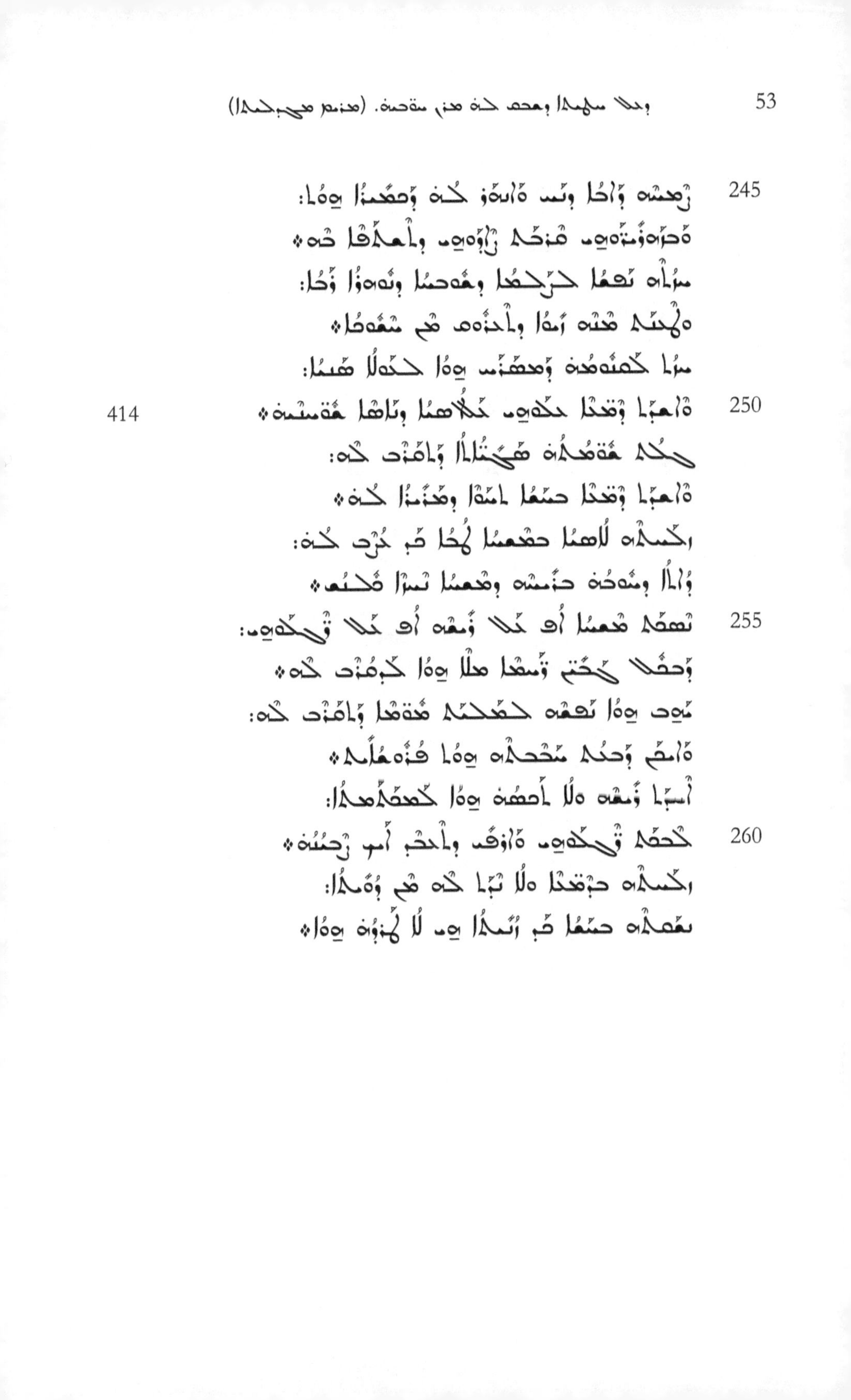

Wherever she wanted she drew near and grabbed [Him] shamelessly.
And because she trembled from [her] love, she was allowed to approach.

The whole Treasury of divinity was let open in front of her, 265
In order that she might be a model in her proximity [to the Lord] for those who repent.

She descended there to the baptismal font so that she might be purified.
If she had been ashamed, she would have left without forgiveness.

Oil and tears she poured out there upon the Holy One,
With the result that the entire ritual of baptism was completed. 270

{415} The excellent oil and the little water were mixed.
The Great High Priest made atonement for the defiled girl by performing His own part. <Heb. 4:14–10:31>

The wise woman knelt before the Forgiver,
In order to come to spiritual birth, which she lacked [lit. because she was deficient].

She bent her head over to wipe His feet with her hair. <Luke 275
7:38; John 12:3>
And just as in baptism she received holiness from the Holy One.

She entered into the second womb, the place of atonement,<John 3:4>
So that in new birth she might become beautiful in a spiritual sense.

She grasped His feet to find a Sea of mercy at the banquet.
She was baptized [lit. dove down] in Him, and He cleaned and 280
polished her, and she arose pure.

She exposed her soul before the Great Flood of holiness.
He poured forth on her waves of His mercy so that she might be atoned.

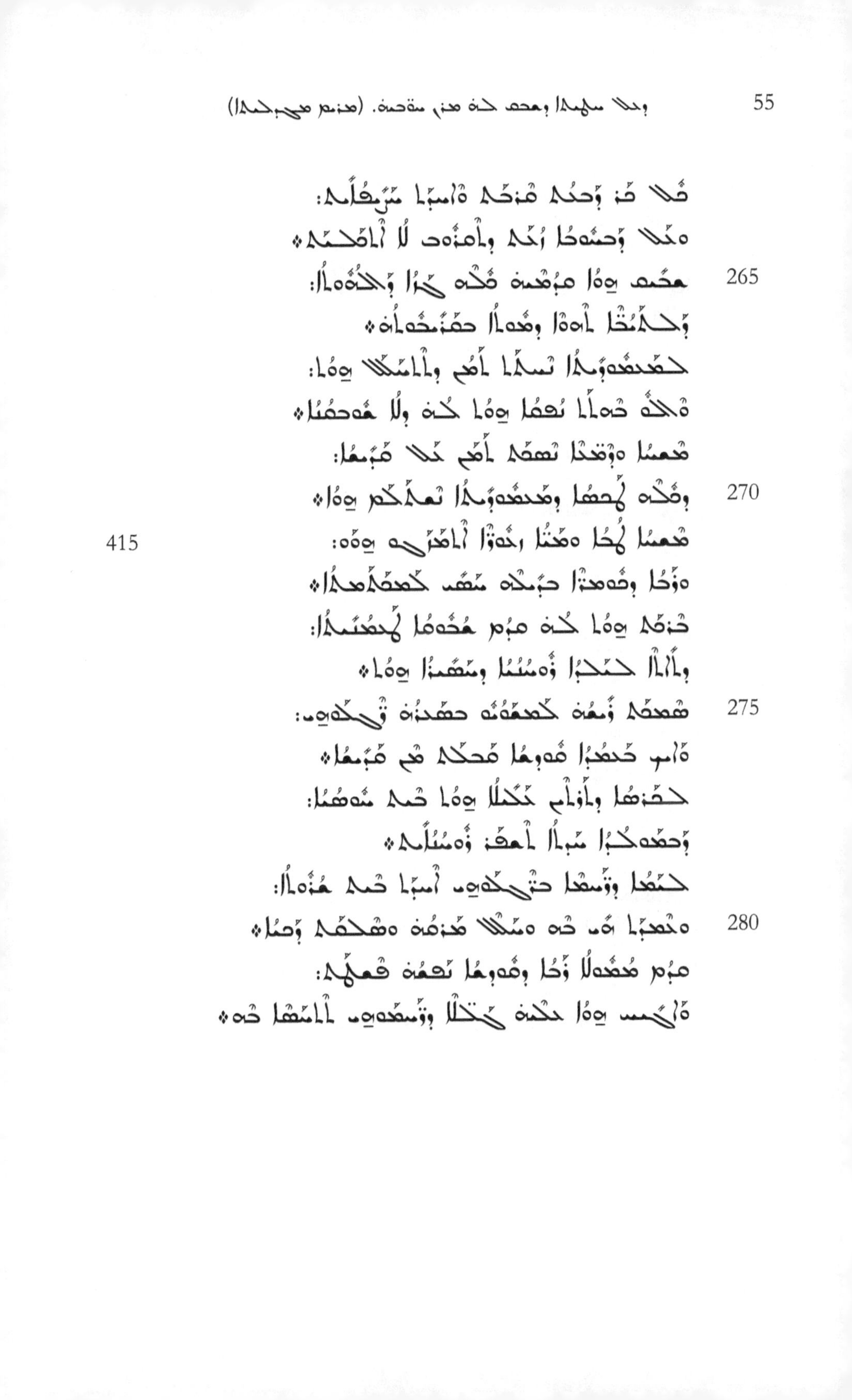

She presented herself to the Living Fire clothed in the body.
It burnt the thicket of her soul and [the evil] vanished completely.

Her love brought [her soul] into the crucible of mercy and smelted it there. 285
Its [refined] gold showed its beauty so that it might be a cast ornament to the Lord of Kings.

The Lord at Simon's Table

Our Lord was reclining to eat the supper of the Pharisee. <Luke 7:36>
His love moved the Sinful Woman so that she might draw near to Him.

He was hungry to forgive because of His mercy which is woven into Him.
And at the banquet of Simon He found what He hungered for [lit. wanted]. 290

{416} They invited Him as a prophet to eat supper.
But He made use of forgiveness like God.

The weeping which He heard from the prostitute was more pleasing to Him.
Than the preparations that Simon brought to present to Him.

The teardrops which He received there were more lovely to Him 295
Than all the drinking that came with the meal.

The sound of the groans that were being poured out was more beautiful to Him
Than what Simon had prepared for the supper.

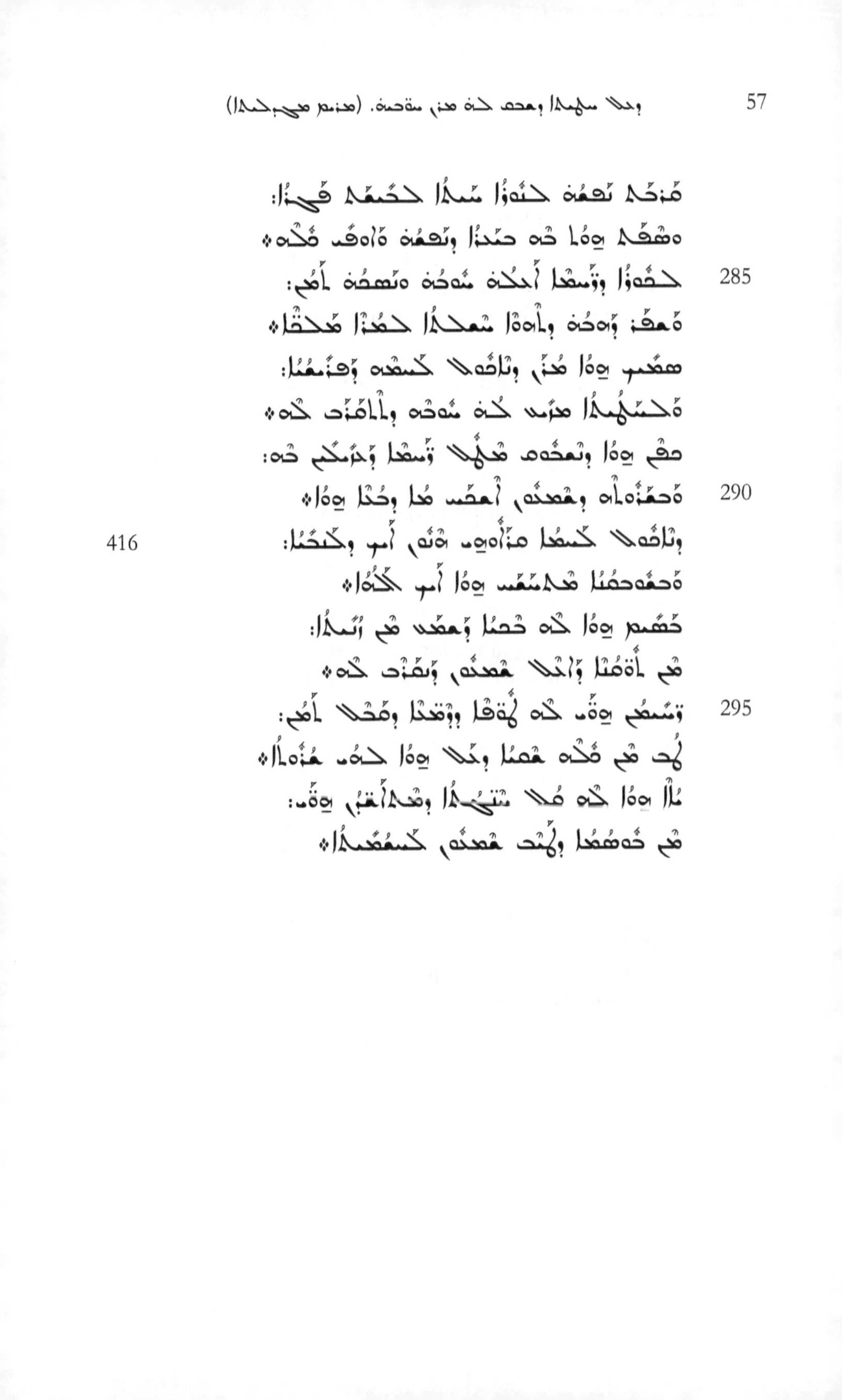

The dinner party asks questions about the food that was set out.
But our Lord gives heed to the prayers which are murmured. 300

Everyone was expecting to get the beverage [lit. to attain the drinking] that will delight him.
But Jesus drinks in the melodies of suffering that are sung unto Him.

They were engrossed in the delicacies that Simon brought in.
[Jesus] was delighted in the repentance which He loves.

He eats with them, but His attention is directed at the prostitute, 305
For He was very hungry for [her] supplication, that it might be presented to Him.

At that time Simon was divided about the True One.
He considered Him ignorant of the things [she] had done.

The ignorance of Simon assailed the Omniscient One, 310
And He was considered to be ignorant of the hidden things.

{417} The ignorant one was doubting the Knower,
Because if He was a prophet He would know (so it says) who approached Him. <Luke 7:39>

Simon understood that the woman who had entered was sinful.
And he did not allow the polluted woman to draw near to himself.

If [Jesus] had been close to divine revelations [so Simon thought] 315
He would have rebuked the polluted woman, and she would have fled from Him.

If He had a secret eye that could see mysteries,
He would have recognized her blemishes for she is so foul.

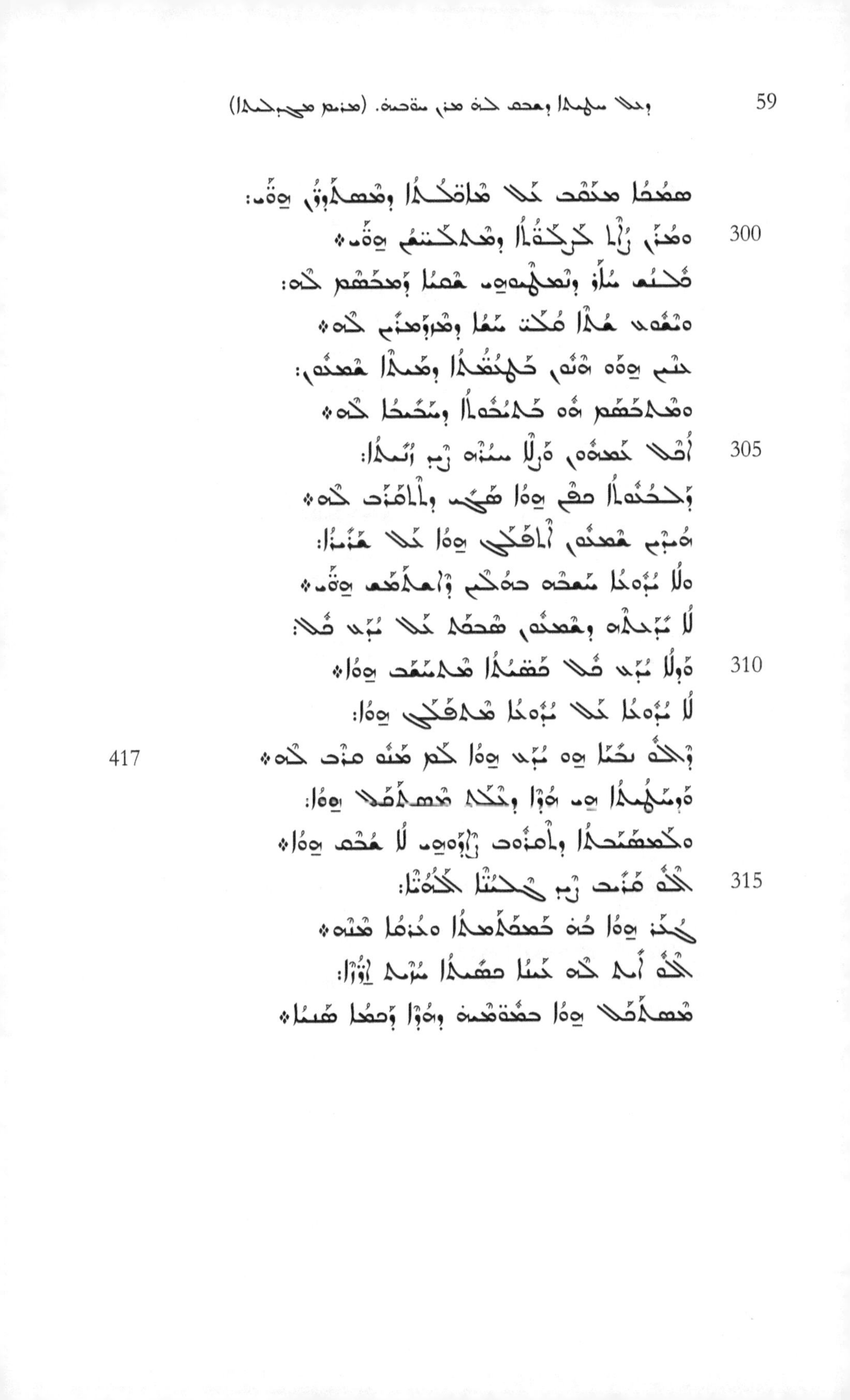

417

If He had an intellect that controlled the hidden things,
He would not give permission to the polluted woman to grasp His feet. 320

It is obvious indeed that He is not at all a prophet;
He did not restrict the Sinful Woman from Himself since He did not recognize her.

Simon seethed with these thoughts for he did not understand.
And he was divided concerning the Omniscient One, whom he himself had invited.

The Good Physician was eager to heal the polluted woman. 325
And He was rejected by the onlookers when He healed [as if] He did not know her.

If He is a prophet He would know (so they say) who this woman is. <Luke 7:39>
And [Simon] would have called Him a prophet only on the strength of [recognizing the woman].

Before his doubts the Pharisee, who had invited [Jesus], called Him a prophet.
But after he had doubted, [Jesus] was considered [by Simon] to be not even a prophet. 330

[Simon's] integrity was divided even when he set out from the start.
{418} Therefore, he was susceptible to the doubt which assailed him.

When [Simon] honored the Lord of the Prophets (by inviting Him), he reckoned [Jesus] a prophet.
[Simon] was divided because the emotion of his love was wanting.

If he had acknowledged from the beginning that the son is the Son, 335
[Certainly] not at the end would he have not even regarded Him as a prophet.

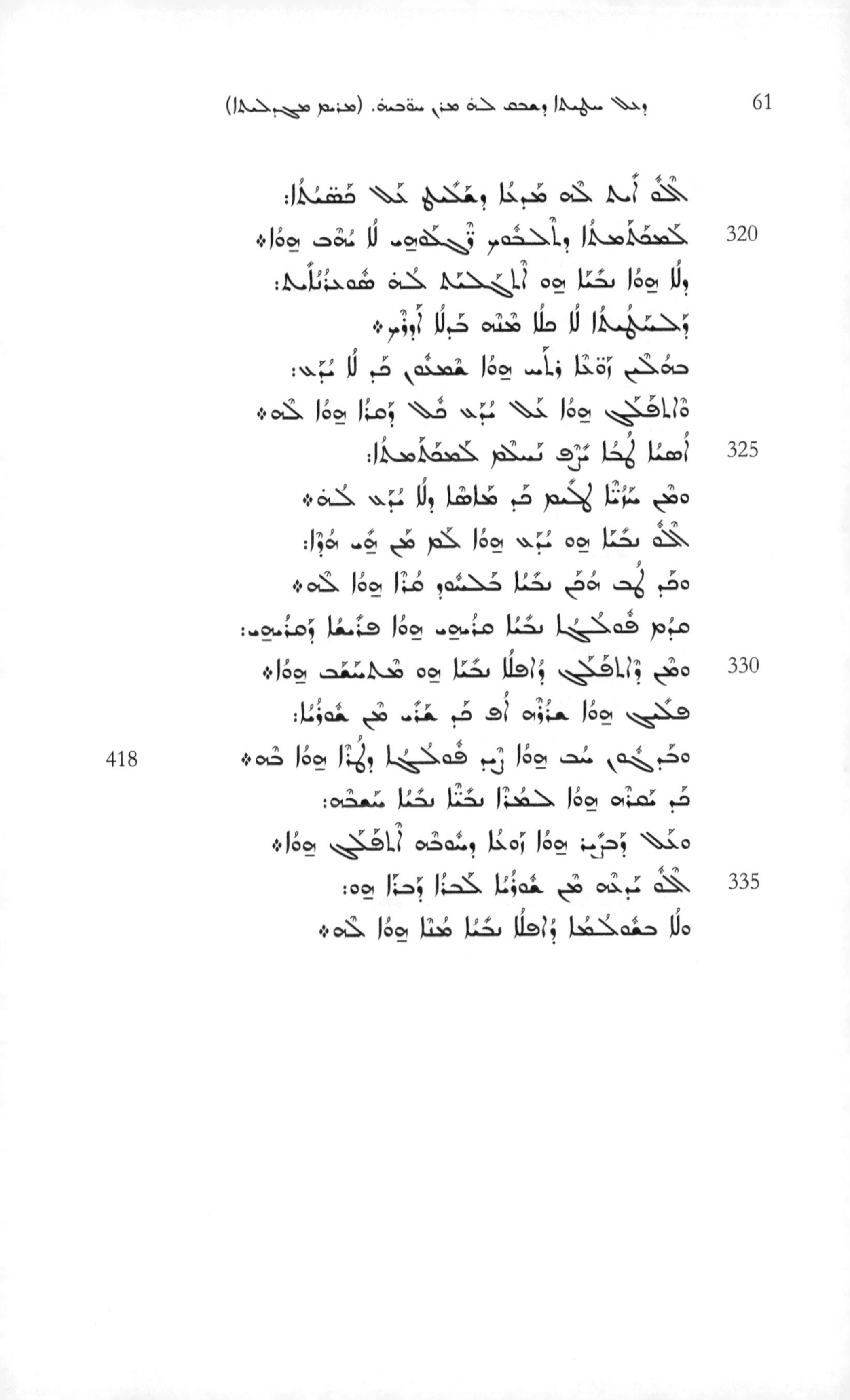

The foundation of his faith was empty.
Therefore it was powerless against doubt when doubt struck it.

"If He is a prophet, He would have known," as one may say, <Luke 7:39>
"For He is not even a prophet, though I supposed that He was a prophet."   340

Simon is Tested

But the Knower turned to Simon calmly:
"I have something to tell you: judge rightly." <Luke 7:40; 7:43>

The Good Shepherd holds His sheep lovingly, <John 10:11–16>
So that when He seeks to find one, He will not lose another. <Matt 12:11–12; 18:12–14; Luke 15:4–6>

He had visited to drive out the offence from [Simon] with various tricks,   345
So that [Simon] might also repent, together with her, that is, the woman He [already] found.

"I have something to tell you," He said.
And Simon answered to our Savior, "Speak, Rabbi." <Luke 7:40>

He caught [Simon] humbly so that he might be judged because he doubted.
But it was lovingly that he himself said to Him, "Speak, Rabbi."   350
<Luke 7:40>

The Wise of Mind made Simon into a judge,
So that he might accuse himself because he was divided concerning the True One.

{419} "There were two debtors to one creditor.
One owed 500 and the other owed 50.

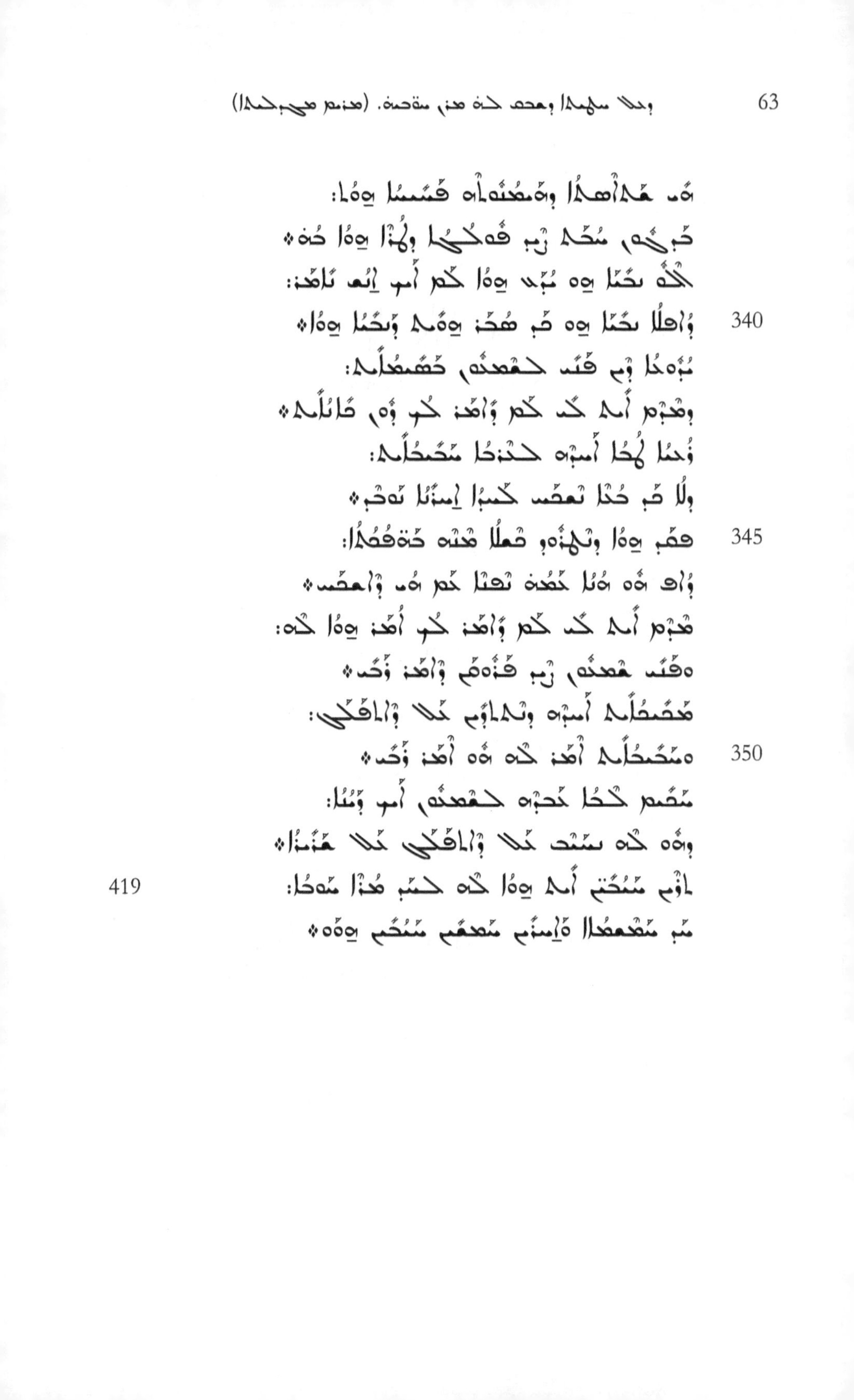

And because they did not have anything to give back to him, he remitted both. 355
Which of these do you say should love him more?" <Luke 7:41–42>

Simon said, "The former should love him more;
His debt is greater than that of his companion.

His love for the remitter should be as great as the remission.
It is appropriate that he love the creditor more." 360

Simon became a judge for his own soul concerning the hidden things.
He did not understand the hidden speech from his own mind.

He accused himself and was proud that he was appointed to make a judgment.
He was not good enough, yet he considered himself a judge.

He entered his verdict and was eager to settle [the case] uprightly. 365
But because the truth surrounded him justly, he emerged guilty.

The judge was judged—he was found guilty by himself—
While thinking that the verdict he entered referred to another.

He entered his verdict and he was found guilty and he emerged not knowing [what had happened].
He became a judge and he accused himself, but he did not understand. 370

He judged rightly, but did not know he would be found guilty,
Lest he exalt himself over the One who knows the hidden things.

Both he and the Sinful Woman were considered the two guilty ones.
{420} He entered an opinion, but by it he was exposed as guilty.

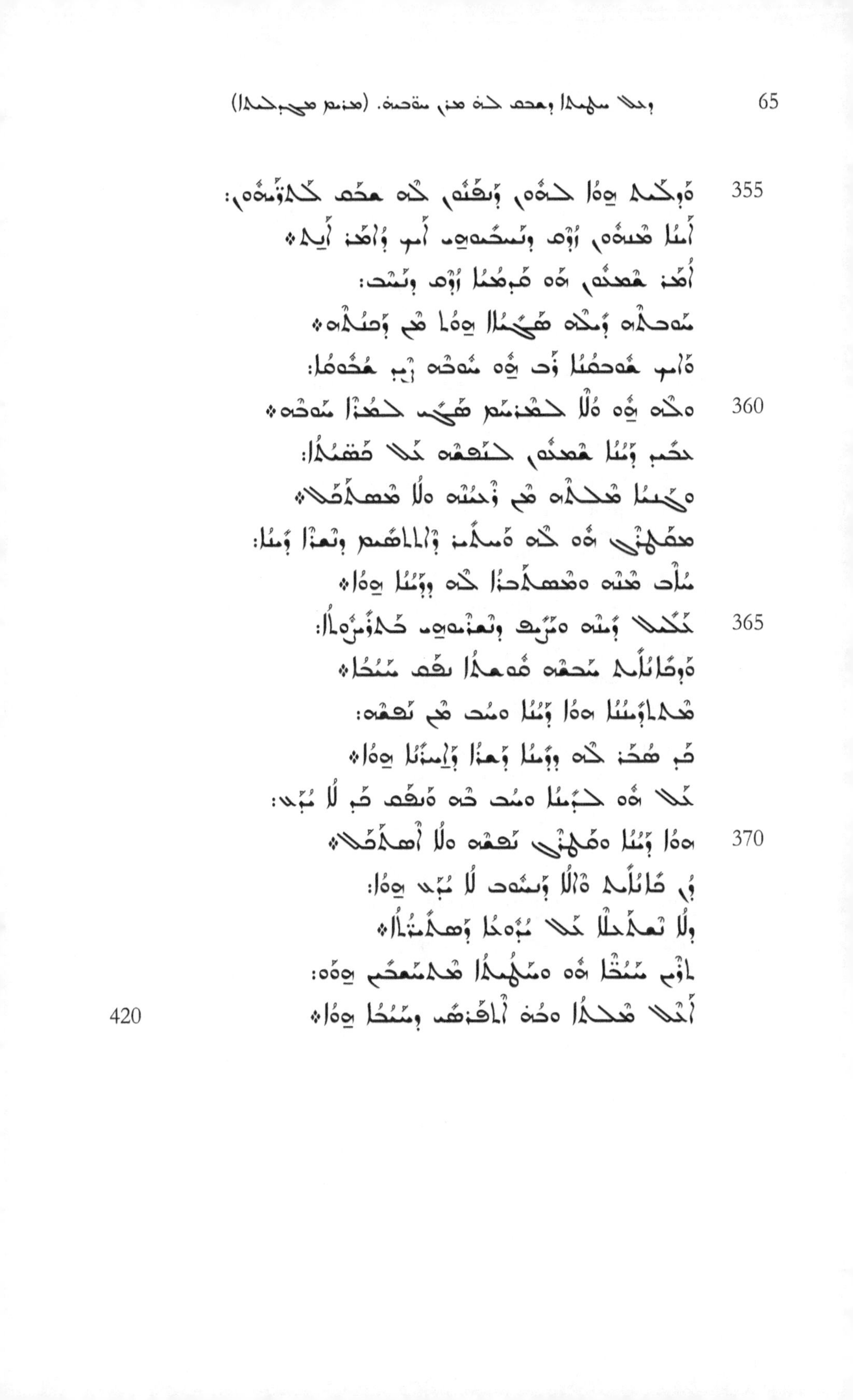

The Wise of Mind trapped him in his words just like David.   375
He was found guilty by his own words, just like the Son of Jesse, when he was asked.

The prophet Nathan condemned David through his responses. <2 Sam 11–12>
And the Lord of Nathan similarly condemned the Pharisee.

The prophet and his Lord judged the king and the Pharisee.
And they condemned them through their own words, when they were interrogated.   380

The judges were judged by their actions.
And they pronounced condemnation for themselves.

The woman full of sins grabbed by His feet the One who is full of compassion.
But when Simon had found fault with her, he was judged wisely.

Our Lord began to explain to him how things really are;   385
And He showed him that the verdict he entered is not another's [but is for Simon himself].

[Jesus] turned His face to the prostitute in great love.
And He began to explain to Simon about her. <Luke 7:44>

He sought to display her great love in the presence of those who were reclining;
[And] how much had her love exceeded the discrimination of   390
the one who had invited Him.

"I entered your house," He had said to the Pharisee.
"But you did not even bring water for my feet, to offer it to me.

But she drenched them discerningly with her tears.
She in truth offered me the very hair of her head instead of a cloth. <Luke 7:44>

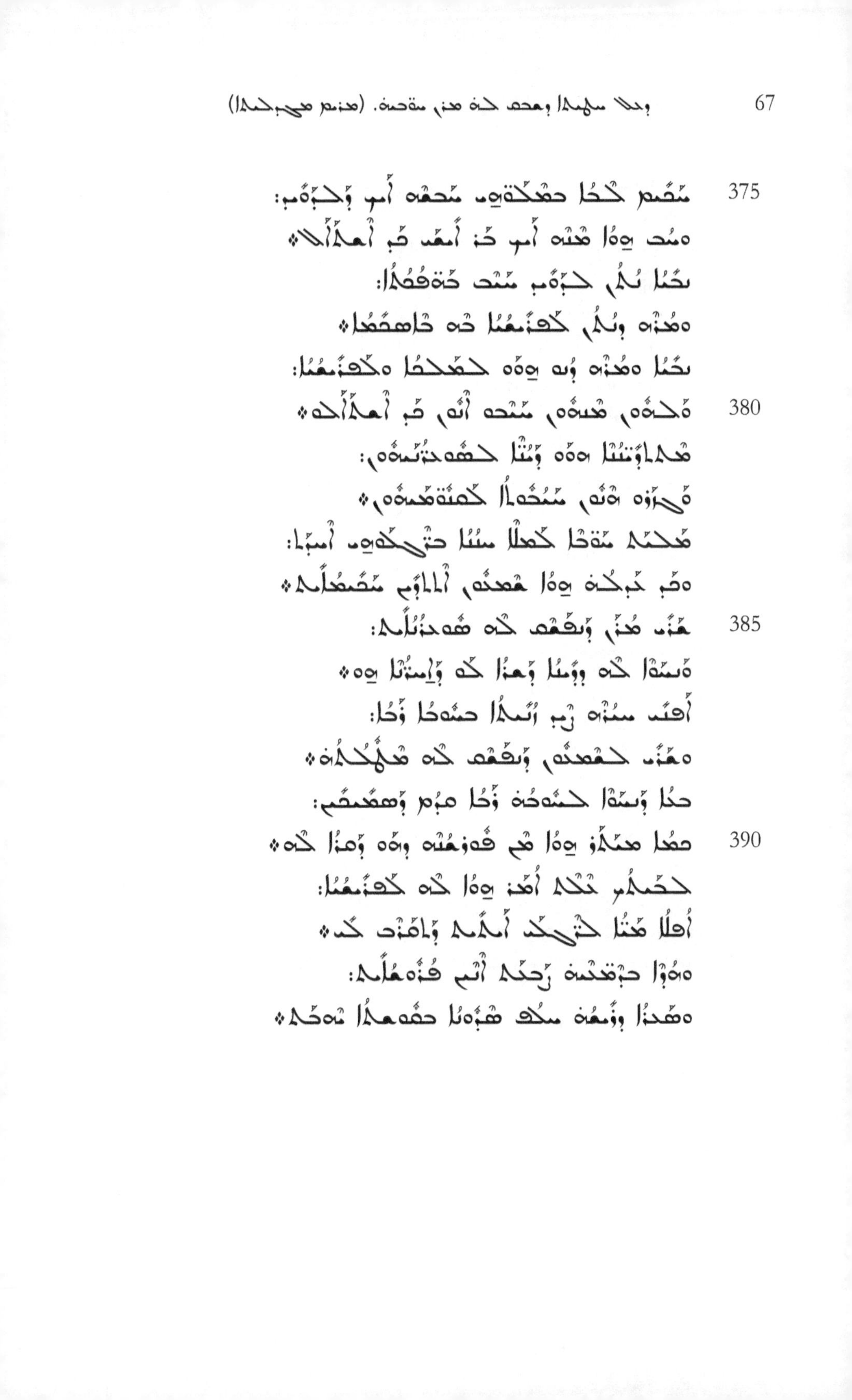

{421} You did not kiss me so that everyone might see the sign of your love, 395
But she did not cease from kissing my feet. <Luke 7:45>

You did not anoint me although it was demanded from your [absent] decorum,
But she sprinkled me lovingly with excellent oil. <Luke 7:46>

Your decorum was far below [lit. very much lighter than] what is acceptable,
But she showed her love to me in many ways. 400

You brought before me a feast of bread and wine,
But she offered her prayer, her tears, her perfume, and her hair.

You mix the kind of thing [i.e. wine] that comes to nothing,
But she kissed my feet all over.

You showed your love in perishable tastes, 405
But she repeated her petition with penitent cries.

Her love is greater than your meal and your delicacies,
And because she loved so much, her sins, which were many, are forgiven." <Luke 7:47>

The Sinful Woman's Conversion

Oh woman, full of blemishes, you whose beauties are many!
I am amazed at you, and how I shall describe you I do not know. 410

Happy mother, who conceived iniquity and gave birth to deceit,
But who in forgiveness gained purity and holiness.

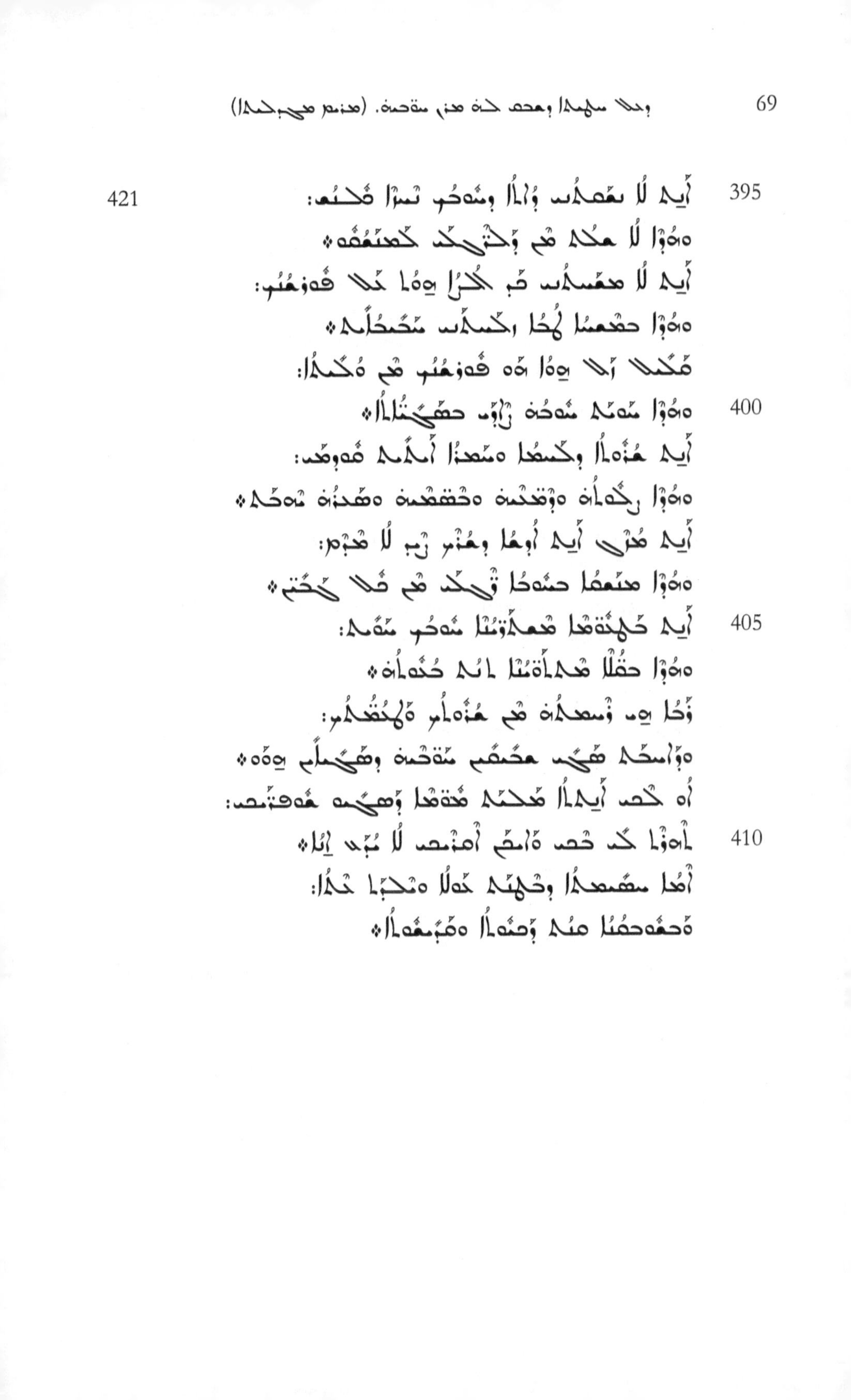

Lover of falsehood, who passed many years in it,
But whose effect is magnified [through the Gospel story], just as the apostles in their preaching. <Mark 14:9; Matt 26:13; 28:18–20>

{422} Mistress of sins, who was polluted by her own deeds, 415
Jesus with His hyssop purified and cleansed her, and she became pure. <Ps 51:7>

Putrid spring, out of whom sprung every kind of evil.
But mercy converted her, and streams which were bitter became sweet. <Exod 15:25>

Troubled of soul, who had become dark through her offences.
Jesus the Light shined and made lucid her gloominess. <John 1:5; 8:12; 9:5> 420

A vulture, who snatched up shamelessly everyone who met her.
Christ the Eagle made her a dove after she saw Him.

A stone, which was a stumbling block of iniquity for every-one who came to her.
But behold! She was set upon the foundation of apostle-ship. <Matt 16:18>

A she-wolf, who approached the Chief Shepherd. 425
But after she saw Him she became a ewe in His field.

A woman, who transgressed through many evil deeds,
Sings lovingly her own name as gospel.

Hater of life, whom iniquity covered most of her days.
But Christ adorned her to become a princess of the beautiful things. 430

All of creation was represented in the defiled woman,
Who through the advent of Jesus became beautiful and pure.

In the oil and tears that she poured out there on the Savior,
She prefigured the baptism of the world for the world symbolically.

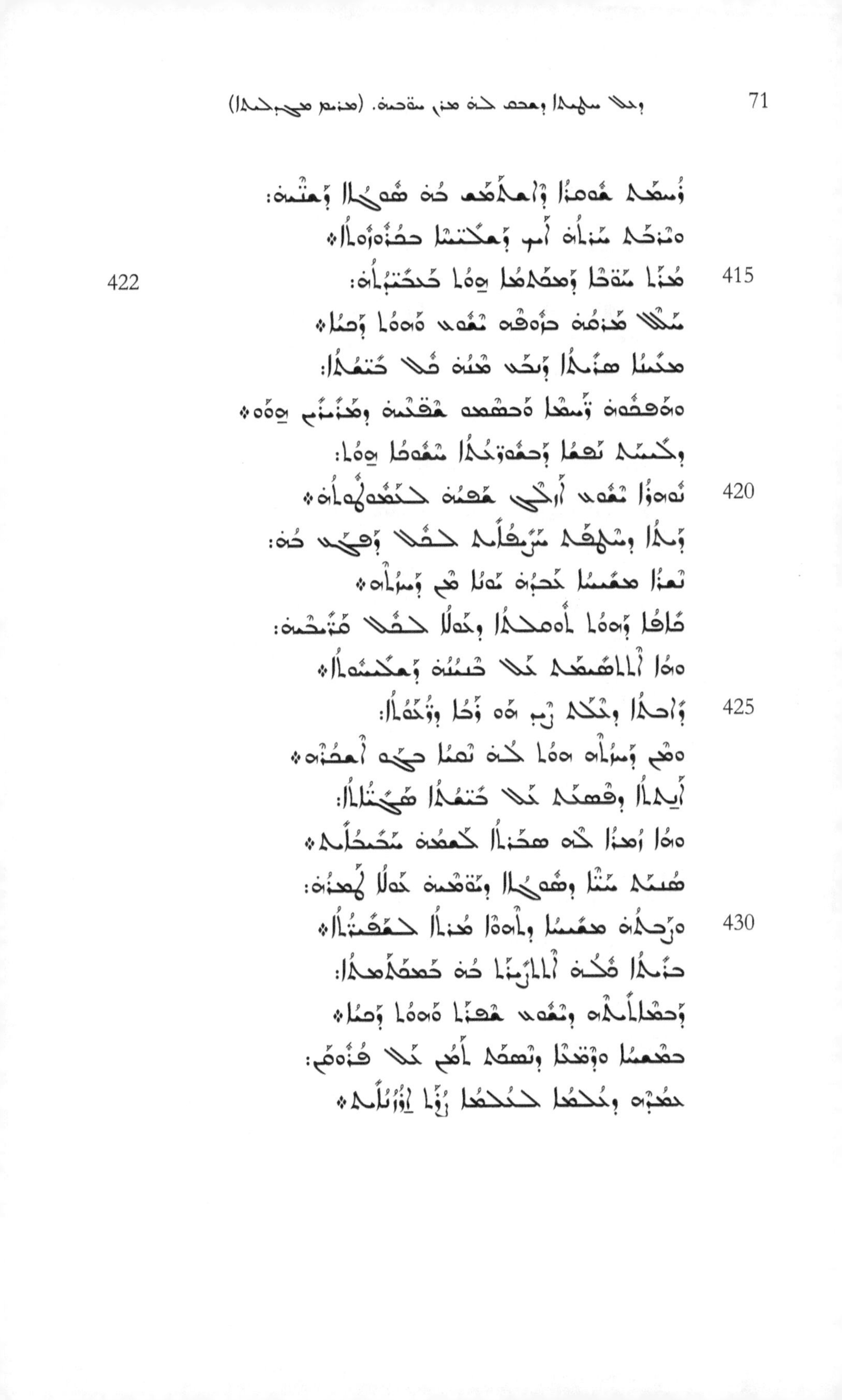

{423} The fragrance of her excellent perfume was scattered over those who were reclining. <John 12:3>   435
The house was exceedingly full of the pleasant smoke. <Gen 8:21>

The nostrils [of those present] fell short [of being able to take in] [lit. from] its fragrance and feared its greatness,
For it blazed up powerfully in the whole house.

Those who were reclining marveled at the sweetness of the excellent oil.
Its novel fragrance, which was abundant, overcame them.   440

The matter of the oil and its choice fragrance alarmed them.
And they began to argue at the table about it.

There was one man who set its value at 300 gold pieces and he claimed that was its worth. <Mark 14:5; John 12:5>
There was another man who said it was worth 200 and asked why it should perish.

Judas had longed for its value because he was a thief.   445
He suggested a high price because he was greedy [lit. his need was excessive]. <John 12:5–6>

The Fragrant Oil

What was the fragrance of the oil that made it so great?
And why was its force [such] that [one suggested] it would go for 300, if not [that, then] for 200?

What spices were crushed into it, or what roots?
Seeing that [the oil] had acquired so great a fragrance and power.   450

Through what [special] force did it capture the apostles who were reclining?
So that just as with great astonishment they would ask why it should perish. <Matt 26:8>

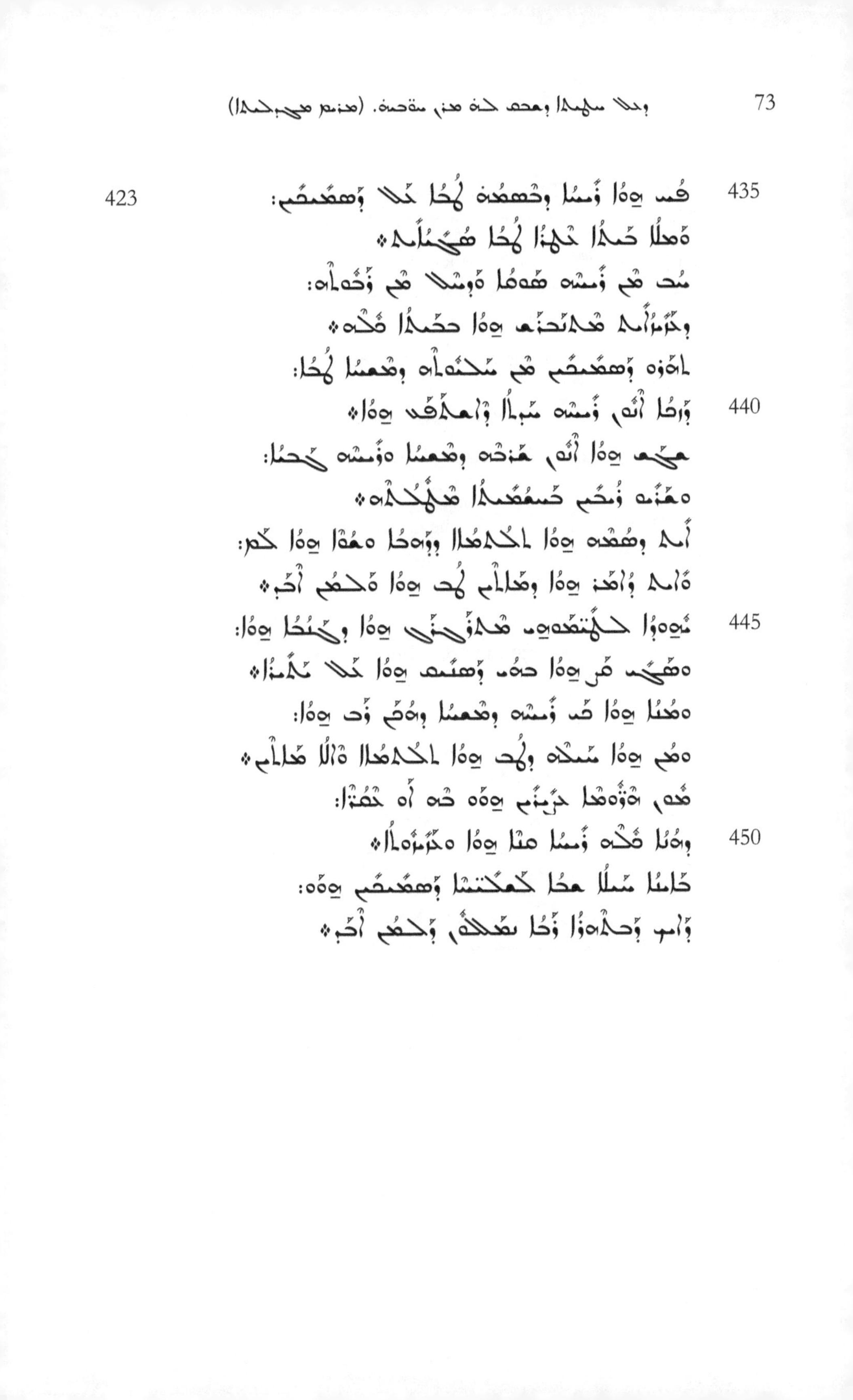

423

From the Great Tree of Life, upon which it fell, <Rev 22:2>
[The oil] took its power and acquired its fragrance and intensity.

{424} The good perfume of the believing woman fell upon Jesus. 455
The fervor and power fell also [lit. were increased] upon those who were reclining.

She had stirred up the Sea of Perfumes when she approached Him.
And excellent incense went up from Him powerfully.

She anointed the holy Christ with oil discerningly,
And a sweet fragrance arose from Him and amazed them. 460

She lit with love the Lord of the Censers lovingly.
He begat an incense so that it might also involve the apostles in the astonishment.

It was from its roots that the oil receives the excellent fragrance
And becomes powerful in accordance with the strength of the ingredients.

Thus, Isaiah called the Messiah a root 465
That would arise from an arid land [i.e. the Virgin] without sexual intercourse. <Isa 53:2>

It was upon this Root of Life that the oil fell,
And it was from Him that [the oil] received its wonderful and ineffable fragrance.

The Son of the Virgin was the Root in the thirsty land,
And He introduced the fragrance into the oil that fell upon 470
Himself.

And although the perfume of the blessed woman was excellent,
It was from the Living One that it acquired the additional element, when it anointed Him.

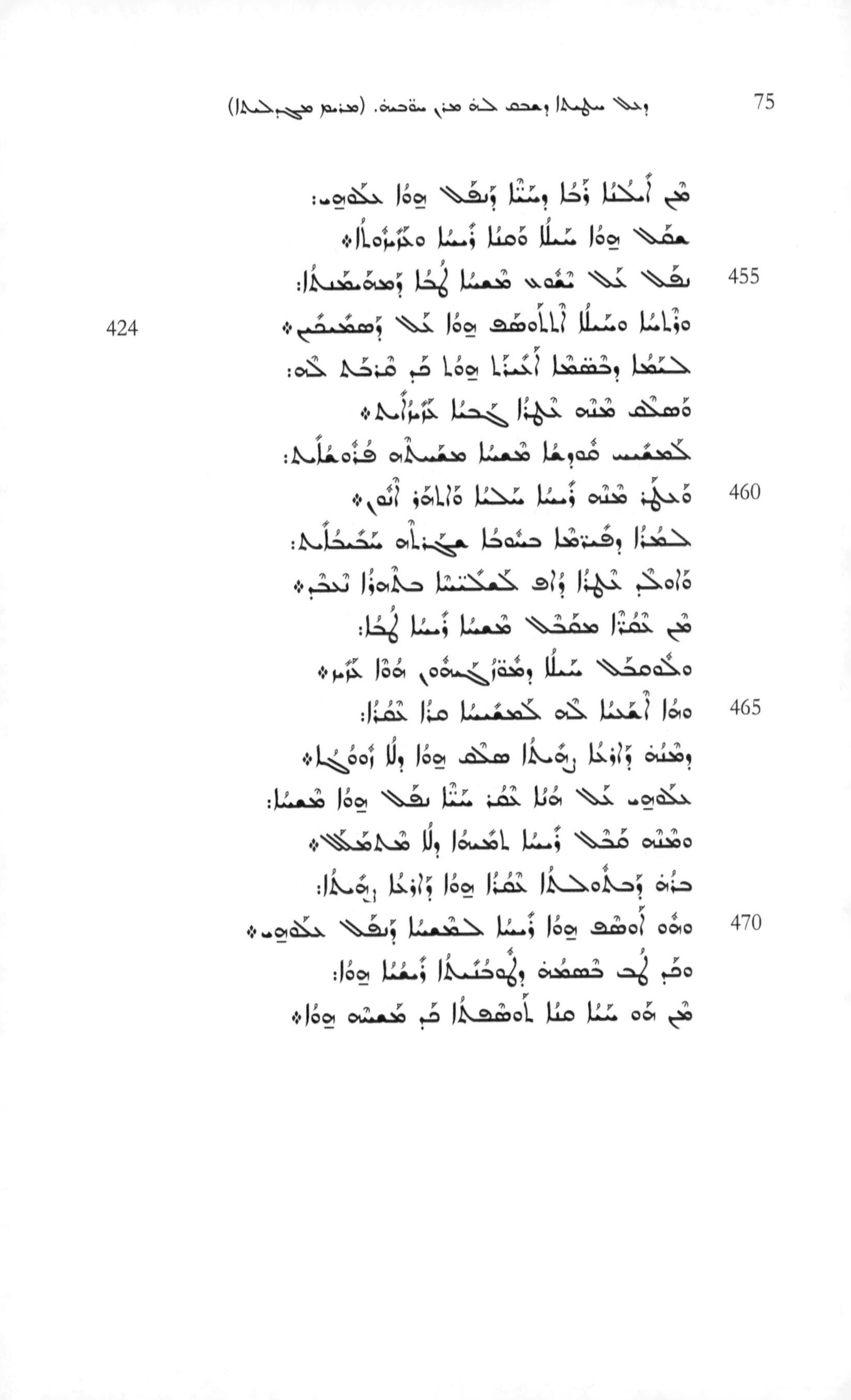

For this reason [i.e. the fragrance], those who were reclining were amazed at the oil
That had no peer in the world which could be as great as *this* one.

{425} It was because of the strength of its choice fragrance that they put a high price on it, 475
For they did not know what to say about it.

Treacherous Judas made use of his habitual trick, <John 12:4–6>
He who was trying to find a way to steal the value of the oil.

"Why was this oil not sold for a lot of money?
Its value would be such as to be beneficial to the poor." <Matt 26:8–9; Mark 14:4–5; John 12:5> 480

When [this] evil will spoke, our Lord restrained it,
So that the utterance which the treacherous one sang out might not be praised.

He said, "Leave her alone. This woman acts according to her will,
And there is also a need for this act [i.e. preparation for burial]. <Matt 26:12; Mark 14:8; John 12:7>

It is the corpse she entered to anoint here, before the [fateful] days. 485
For after I am crucified, no one will anoint or put balsam on me.

Oil is useful for the day of my burial and, behold, this is from today.
She did this while there is an opportunity [given] by [my] crucifiers.

The deadly sword has not yet come to scatter you [disciples] away. <Zech 13:7; Matt 26:31; John 16:32>
She has anointed me because after you have fled no one will. 490

Behold, she is laboring instead of you before the event.
Let her do that which was your task to fulfill.

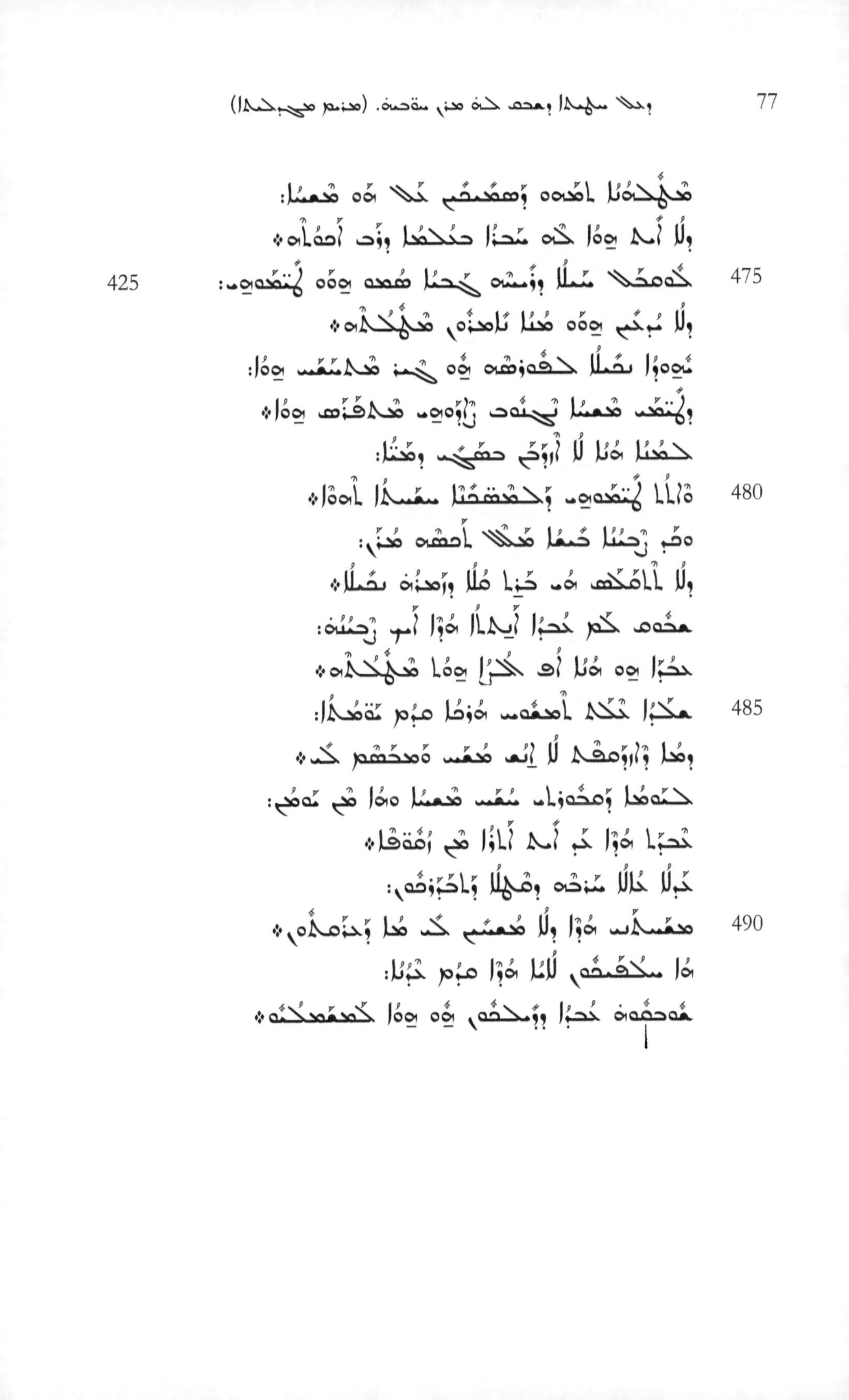

It is a beautiful act that she performed for me, because I am slain.

It is the order that she fulfilled, she who will not at all be slighted by me.

For this reason her story will go out into the whole world. 495

And with my gospel her remembrance will shine out." <Mark 14:9; Matt 26:13>

{426} Our Lord healed all of the blemishes which were near to Him.

He healed in His compassion the iniquity of the soul and the diseases of the body. <Ps 103:3>

He cleansed the Pharisee's body from its marks,

And He cured the prostitute's soul because she was sick. 500

It is the former from his leprosy and the latter from her evil deeds,

[Whom] He cleansed and forgave both hidden iniquity and manifest leprosy. <Mark 14:3; Matt 26:6>

Her soul and his body were purified;

He who is a Great Physician and Forgiver met with both of them.

He forgave the 500 and He forgave the 50 because He is 505 compassionate.

[He forgave] the soul its iniquity and the body its leprosy, which was scarred.

The debtors even paid Him back [lit. repaid Him recompenses] for their forgiveness.

They weighed out and gave to Him [their] love instead of their debt-contracts.

He, whose manifest leprosy was cleansed, honored the Lord manifestly.

And in his visible preparations he made a banquet.[3] 510

---

[3] The banquet that was condemned now is praised.

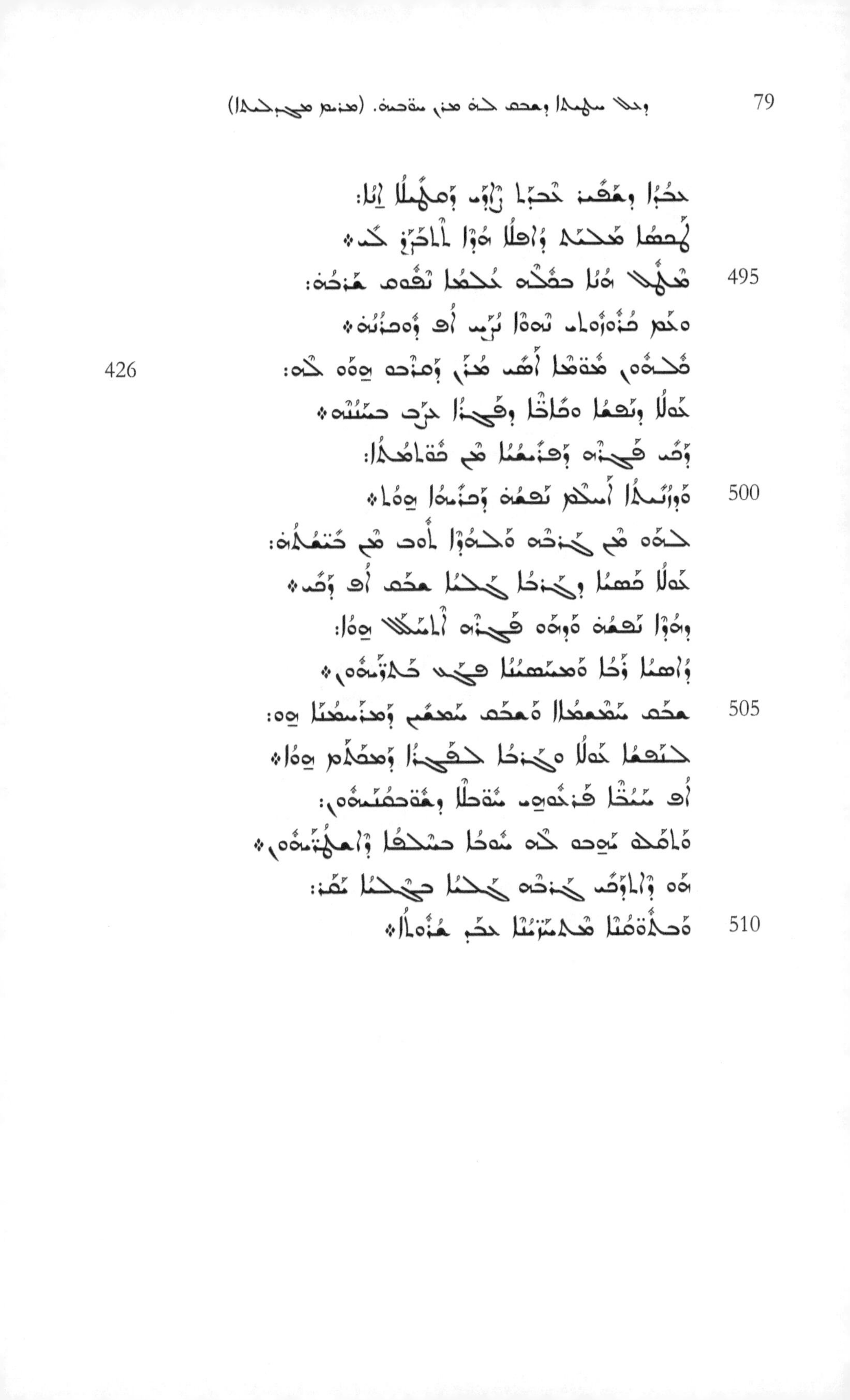

426

She, whose secret iniquity was atoned, loved Him secretly.
And with groans, passion, and tears she sought forgiveness.

And the Compassionate One gave forgiveness to both of them.
The former He cleansed and the latter He atoned, because [they both] sought Him.

Cry Tears of Repentance

Not even today is His treasury lacking in forgiveness. 515
It is full just as it has always been, and its door will be opened for the one who seeks Him.

{427} Whoever has pains in his body should run unto Him.
And whoever iniquity of the soul has marked should take shelter in Him.

Bring tears, just like the prostitute, to the house of God.
And receive, just like her, forgiveness of sins for yourselves. 520

Kiss His gates and draw near to His threshold, just as she did.
And sprinkle with your tears the ground of the house of atonement.

It is here [in the house of atonement] that Jesus is the one loved by the prostitute.
And He stands ready to forgive hidden sins for those who invite Him.

He who is needing forgiveness for his deeds, 525
Let him sprinkle tears on His threshold and, behold, he is forgiven.

He who is bitten by the serpent who killed Adam, <Gen 3:15>
Let him drink the cup of Jesus, who conquered [the serpent's] poison. <Rom 5:12–21; Heb 2:14>

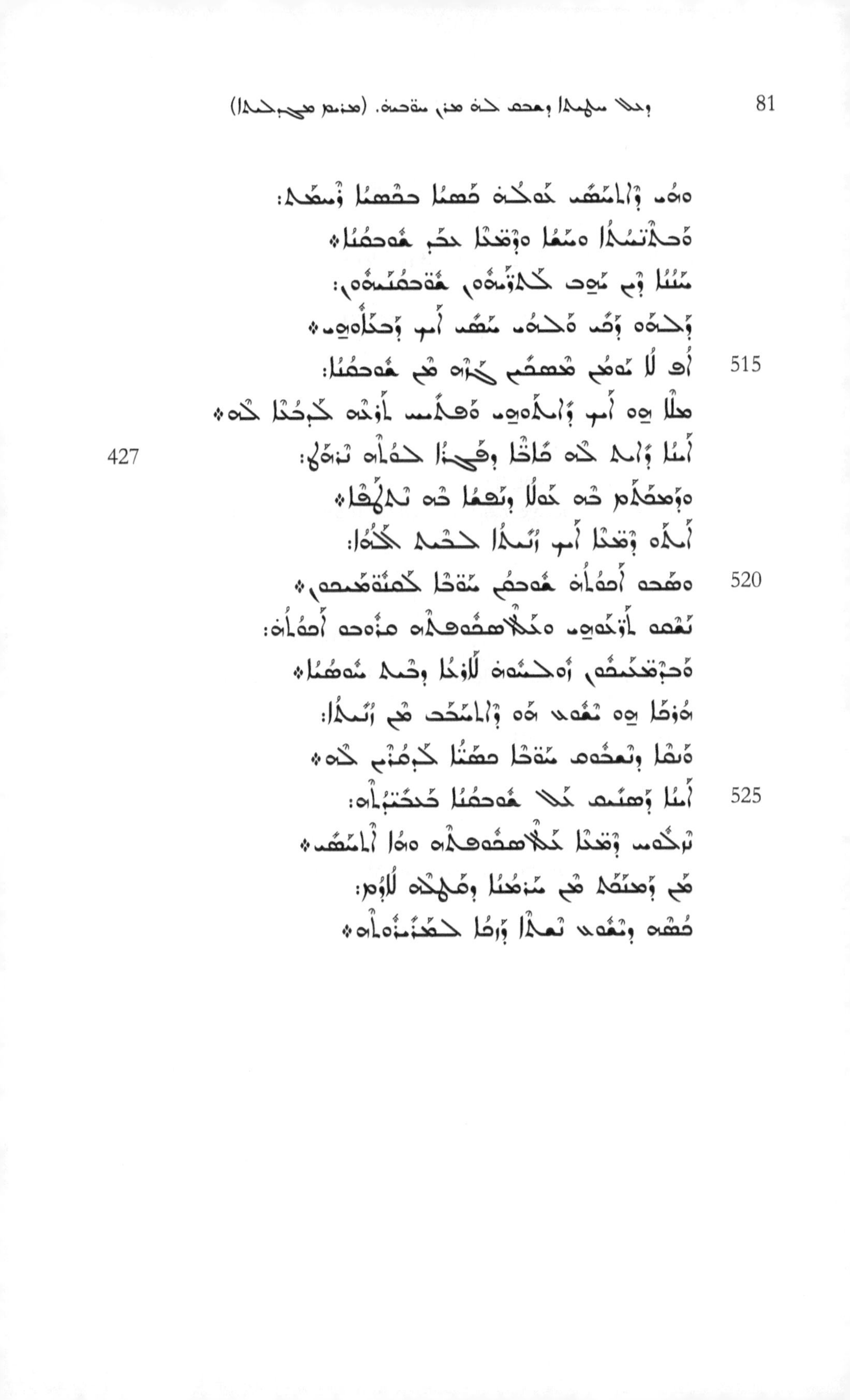

He who has made a mark on his soul through free-will,
He has a Physician who will freely heal him. 530

He who willfully went astray and fell, let him also wish to stand up.
For it is your choice to run your course according to your wish.

Make a petition, just like the Sinful Woman, and bring it to Him.
For in Him is His mercy every day and every moment. <Lam 3:22–23>

Weep just as she wept, loving as she loved, 535
And you will receive from the Giver the same atonement as hers.

Jesus is today and He was yesterday and will always be. <Heb 13:8>
Just as He forgave, He will also forgive the one who seeks Him.

{428} His gate is open and His love is poured out to the penitent one. <John 10:1–10>
Blessed is the Compassionate One, the story of whose mercy 540
cannot be contained. <John 21:25>

The end of the *memra* on the Sinful Woman
which was spoken by Mar Jacob.

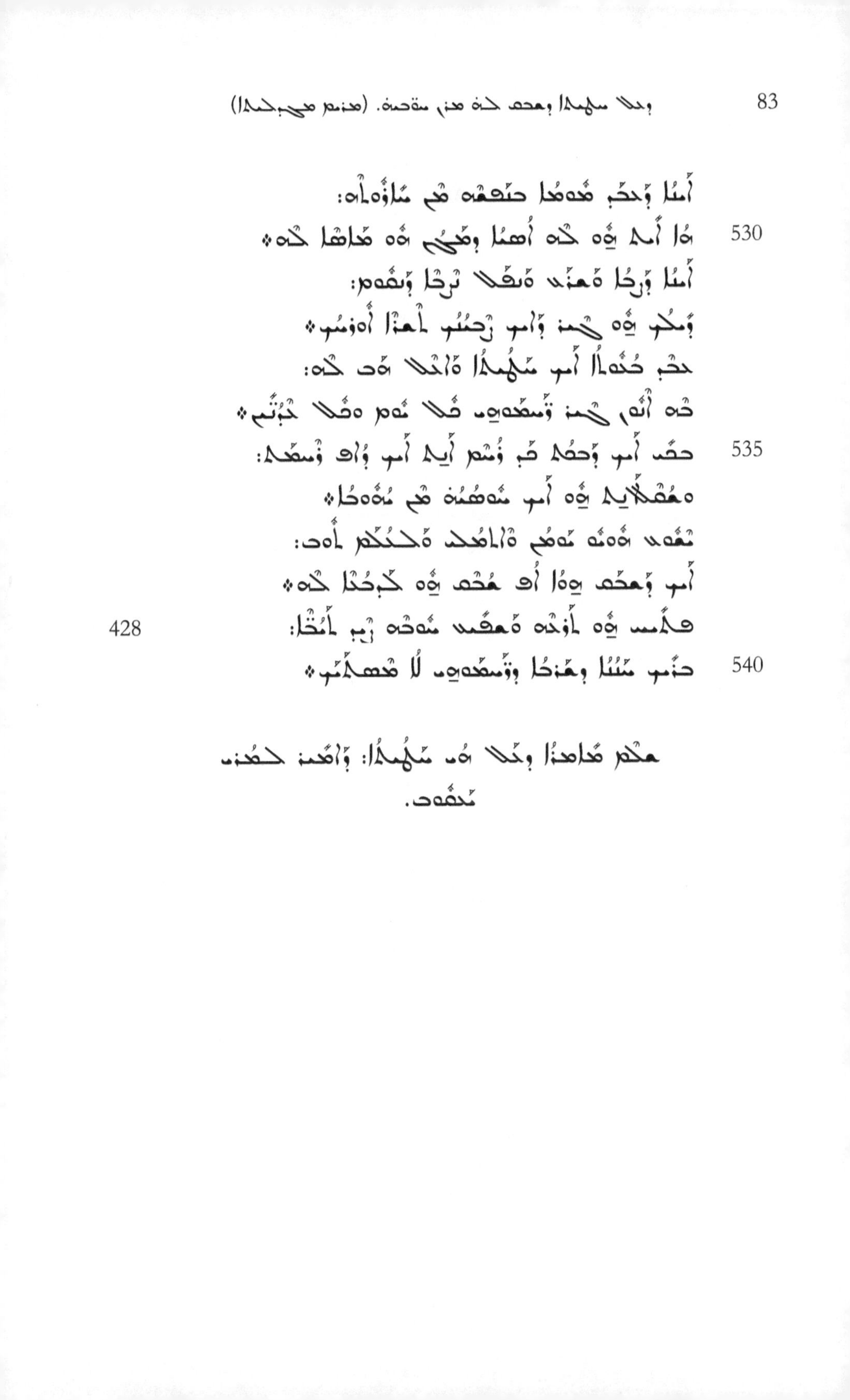

أَ:

APPENDIX: ROMANOS AND THE SYRIAC VERSE TRADITION ON THE SINFUL WOMAN

I. INTRODUCTION

Lucas van Rompay's 1993 article, "Romanos le mélode: Un poète syrien à Constantinople," is an attempt to show connections between Romanos and the Syriac tradition by emphasizing Romanos' Syrian origins. On the basis of his analysis of the many themes in Genesis for which the poet's interpretation seems characteristically Syriac, van Rompay claims that "l'exclusion de la tradition syriaque est très discutable" (Rompay 1993, 292). He emphasizes Romanos' upbringing in Emesa and his subsequent training in Beirut, cities which were both part of a "région bilingue" and which both "constitue le charactère distinctif de la Syrie à cette époque" (Rompay 1993, 292–293).[1] He claims specifically that it is wrong to separate Romanos from "la tradition éphrémienne" since the same Syrian Christian environment inspired both Ephrem and Romanos despite the temporal and spatial distance between them, and they both, "dans leur art créatif, ont exploité [la synthèse culturelle] d'une façon personnelle" (Rompay 1993, 293). Theologically speaking, Romanos maintained "le monophysisme populaire" that he grew up with in Syria, according to van Rompay, and the poet was able to keep close contacts with the Syrian community which existed in Constantinople (Rompay 1993, 295–296). Ultimately, Romanos' poetry cannot be understood without reference to "une grande complexité culturelle" that included both Syriac and Greek elements in the sixth century (Rompay 1993, 296).

---

[1] On the chronology of Romanos' poems, see the still-fundamental Maas 1906; and 1910; see also the collected work of Maas's contemporary Karl Krumbacher on Romanos (Krumbacher 1907). Good translations of Romanos abound: in English, Carpenter 1970–1972, Lash 1995, Schork 1995; in French, Grosdidier de Matons 1964–1981; in German, Koder 2005; in Italian, Maisano 2002.

Van Rompay's viewpoint is the standard one today among Syriac scholars, but it needs to be defined more precisely because so few studies of Syriac influence on Romanos have actually been conducted in earnest. The present Appendix represents a brief attempt to consider how the *kontakion* on the Sinful Woman reveals Romanos' engagement with Syriac poems, particularly the Ephremic homily and the anonymous *soghitha* on the Sinful Woman. I discussed above, in my Introduction to the translation, the continuities and discontinuities between Romanos' *kontakion* and Jacob's *memra* on the same theme, as well as Jacob's engagement with these same Syriac poems. Here I will take up Romanos' knowledge of the other two Syriac poems, to ascertain whether there was direct knowledge of these poems outside of Romanos' engagement with Jacob.

As I discussed above, Romanos occasionally draws from Syriac writings that do not share the biblical passage on which he is writing; these appropriations, however, are often hard to locate: I suggested one such appropriation in Romanos' poem *On Repentance* above. Thus, for the purposes of this study it is reasonable to begin with the most obvious potential sources, that is, the Syriac poems that share the theme of the Sinful Woman. I have confined my study here to poetry as a way of limiting the material, and Romanos would arguably have gone to the Syriac poetic tradition first for inspiration in composing his own poem. Such an approach, however, naturally excludes the prose texts that I referenced above in my Introduction to the translation. Given the large amount of extant late antique exegesis in both prose and verse on the gospel passages in question, a complete study of all the eastern Christian traditions regarding the Sinful Woman would be a huge and complex task. Here I hope only to add one piece to that larger puzzle.

II. NOTE ON THE TEXT OF THE EPHREMIC *MEMRA* ON THE SINFUL WOMAN

The manuscripts for the *memra* on the Sinful Woman attributed to Ephrem were described by Edmund Beck in the introduction to the second volume of his edition and translation of Ephrem's sermons (1970, 1.ix–x; 1970, 2.x–xii). There are only two surviving manuscripts of the Syriac text, both of which can be found in the British Library.[2] The first, which Beck labeled A,

---

[2] Add. 14651 (Wright 1870–1872, 3.1102) and Add. 17266 (Wright 1870–1872, 2.865).

is the oldest, dating to the mid-ninth century.³ The second (B) dates to the twelfth. There is also an undated Arabic translation in Syriac script (Karshuni) that Beck made use of in the notes (G); he did so especially towards the end of the *memra* where corruptions in A and B are more numerous. A Greek translation of this *memra* also exists, but after the first several lines it diverges sharply from the Syriac text. Consequently, and because the Greek text was not then properly edited, Beck chose not to use it in the apparatus.⁴

Beck was constrained in editing the two Syriac manuscripts by the rules laid down by René Draguet, former editor of the Corpus Scriptorum Christianorm Orientalium.⁵ Draguet stipulated that all CSCO volume editors were to print only one manuscript as their principal text and then to note variations in the apparatus, regardless of the total number of manuscripts available. For this *memra* Beck chose to print A because he ultimately thought it retained more of the original homily. The text of B also often betrays corruption and would have created more problems than A as a principal text. B, however, contains two long sections that A does not: these additions, coming after lines 271 and 297, respectively, make the narrative more coherent and probably at least resemble original material. Beck's solution was to print A and to note B's variations in the apparatus, as stipulated by Draguet, but then to include the two extra sections from B as appendices.

Beck made no unqualified pronouncement on the authenticity of this text. Many of the *memre* originally attributed to Ephrem have been shown to be later imitations, and to some degree scholars must read the works of "Ephrem and his School" as one corpus (Petersen 1985b, xxxii; McVey 1989, 4 n. 6). Beck suggested that at least a kernel ("ein Kern") of the *memra* on the Sinful Woman is original and that A contains the most representative characteristics of Ephrem's work. He pointed to parallels between this *memra* and some verses of the *Carmina Nisibena* that mention Satan's frustration over the Sinful Woman's repentance (60.1–8), verses which he thought presaged the prominent role of Satan in the *memra*. He also

---

³ The full title of this *memra*, found only in A is ܡܚܐܕܐ ܘܣܝܡ ܠܛܘܒܢܐ ܡܪܝ ܐܦܪܝܡ ܥܠ: ܚܛܝܬܐ ܕܐܬܬܘܝܬ ܚܣܝܡܐܝܬ "A *memra* that was Set Down by the Blessed Master Ephrem on the Sinful Woman who was Distressed over her Sin."

⁴ The text remains unedited; for the manuscript data, see *CPG* 2.3952, duplicated at 2.4046.

⁵ Draguet later summarized these rules in print (1977).

suggested that while the ending of A seems somewhat compressed, the text betrays no shortening or mutilation ("nicht etwa geweltsam verkürtz und verstümmelt"). The non-truncated compression of the last scene is not retained by B, where the story is more elaborated and generally smoother. Thus, Beck argues that A is the manuscript that retains a more authentic text because of its status as the *lectio difficilior* as well as its apparent relation to Ephrem's other works.

III. ROMANOS AND THE EPHREMIC *MEMRA* ON THE SINFUL WOMAN

As noted, many of the writings attributed to Ephrem the Syrian seem not to be genuine, but among those considered original there exist a large number of homiletic works.[6] They are in both prose and verse; the latter fall into two categories. 1) *Madrashe* are lyric poems in stanzas that can be written in a variety of syllabic meters: Ephrem uses some fifty meters which range widely in their complexity; 2) *Memre* are narrative poems written in couplets of a standard 7+7 syllabic meter. This form became known as "the meter of Mar [Master] Ephrem" and was commonly used in later Syriac poetry. Ephrem employed both the *memra* and the *madrasha* for verse homilies that typically retell a biblical (sometimes apocryphal) story through dialogues between the principal characters. Later writers also took up these forms, and thus a substantial corpus of verse homilies has survived, extending in date from Ephrem's fourth-century creations through the medieval period.

One of the common features of the verse homily is the presence of dialogue. In a paper delivered to the 4th Symposium Syriacum in 1984, Sebastian Brock distinguished between five different types of "dialogue poem" in Syriac (Brock 1987a). While his types I, II, and III are mostly *soghyatha*—that is, *madrashe* with simple stanzaic patterns (see below)—types IV and V are "exclusively" *memre* (137).[7] Type IV poems have a bare

---

[6] For a summary of the authentic writings of Ephrem, see Brock 1997, 22–28, Beck 1960, and Beck 1962. For a detailed overview of the modern editions of Ephrem, see Melki 1983. Most of the works that purport to be Greek or Latin translations of Ephrem's writings are later pseudonymous creations: on the "tangled corpus" (Brock's phrase) of "Ephrem Graecus" and "Ephrem Latinus," see Hemmerdinger-Iliadou and Kirchmeyer 1960; see also the short bibliography in the notes of Sidney Griffith's 1997 Père Marquette Lecture (38–40 n.6).

[7] Brock has suggested more recently that his typology should be seen as a chronological development (i.e. from I to V), with the earliest *kontakia*

narrative framework into which the dialogues are inserted. The voice of the homilist is left out of the body of the poem but can appear briefly in the prologue and sometimes in an epilogue. Type V poems are basically type IV poems with sections interspersed throughout the narrative wherein the poet can interject a moral, interpret a biblical passage, or address the characters directly. Brock suggested that Ephrem's *memra* on the Sinful Woman belongs to type IV because of its lack of homiletic comment within the narrative (1987a, 142).

As Brock pointed out in comparing these types to what is found in Greek literature of the period, a number of Romanos' *kontakia* can be shown to follow the pattern of types III, IV, and V in their dialogues and narrative structure (1987, 144–145).[8] Paul Maas in his 1910 article on the origins of the *kontakion* had suggested that the simple *madrasha*—corresponding to Brock's type III—was the Syriac form that lay behind the development of Greek hymnography (78–80), and José Grosdidier de Matons, who generally tended to deny a Syriac background to Romanos' *kontakia*, had (here at least) agreed with him, saying, "en ce qui concerne la forme, le *madrasha* se rapproche plus du *kontakion* que la *memra*" (1977, 17).[9] Brock, however, claims that the situation is more complex than Maas's or Grosdidier de Matons's formulations allow, particularly in that both the *madrasha* and *memra* (in their own ways) influenced Romanos: he had suggested that, while on a formal level the *kontakion* probably has taken more from the *madrasha*, thematic material from fourth and fifth century

---

corresponding to the *madrasha* or the *soghitha* (types I–III), "not only in the metrical form (as Maas indicated), but also in the way they handle dialogue" (Brock 1989, 143). Later *kontakia* developed the capacity to incorporate dialogue in other ways, such as by introducing it into the narrative, as the *memra* does (types IV and V).

[8] The type III dialogue poem is a *madrasha* with either a complex or simple stanzaic pattern that includes more than two characters and covers the entire narrative of the episode; see Brock 1987a, 136–137.

[9] De Halleux, in his review of Grosdidier de Matons's monograph, felt that he was here reacting specifically to the views of C. Emereau, "qui insistait sur la dette de Romanos vis-à-vis de l'hymnographie syriaque jusqu'à nier équivalemment la créativité du génie byzantin"; for this quote and further comparisons, see de Halleux 1978, 639–641.

memre is prominent in Romanos' hymns (1987a, 145–146).[10] In stating his case for this double borrowing Brock cautioned that influence of form and influence of content often become confused in discussions of the impact of Syriac literature on Greek hymnography: some themes, such as that of the Sinful Woman, are treated in many forms of Syriac poetry as well as in prose, and these themes seem to appear in Romanos regardless of their original form.[11]

At the beginning of the section on Ephrem in his *The Diatessaron and Ephrem Syrus as Sources of Romanos the Melodist* (1985b), William Petersen reminds the reader of Grosdidier de Matons's judgment on Ephrem's viability as a thematic source for Romanos: "after examining four of Romanos' hymns against several works from Ephrem's corpus, [Grosdidier de Matons] stated 'rien n'indique que Romanos ait eu le texte d'Ephrem sous le yeux.' Let us consider the evidence before rendering a judgment on [this] assertion."[12] Petersen then proceeds to suggest twenty-one "agreements" between the writings of Romanos and Ephrem that he thinks contradict Grosdidier de Matons's assertion. In locating these parallels he claims to be resisting the temptation to collect mere "echoes," citing (among others) Grosdidier de Matons himself and Rodney Schork (a student of Paul Maas) as two scholars who have too readily found in Romanos Greek patristic quotations.[13] Petersen claims that many of the

---

[10] From a more strictly hymnographic point of view, Wellesz (1961, 184) and Werner (1959–1984, 1.227) both diverge from Maas by pointing to the *memra* as the primary influence on Romanos' *kontakia*.

[11] In a more recent article that post-dates the publication of William Petersen's book (1985b), Brock has refined his descriptions of Syriac poetry by proposing a three-fold distinction pertaining to borrowings between Greek and Syriac (1989). He suggests that the evidence from the Syriac *memre* and *madrashe* betrays a distinction between not only metrical form and literary motif but also between these two and what he calls "literary form." In relation to Romanos' use of Syriac literature, Brock suggests that the metrical form that is most influential is "undoubtedly" the *madrasha*, but with regard to the literary form and literary motif both the *memre* and *madrashe* have an impact.

[12] Petersen 1985b, 173, quoting Grosdidier de Matons 1977, 254. It should be noted that Grosdidier de Matons readily acknowledged his ignorance of the Syriac language (1977, 254 n. 57).

[13] Petersen criticizes Schork in particular, whom he suggests did not contribute very much in his thesis to what had already been collected by Krumbacher,

"probable" or "possible" parallels that these authors have found "are not verbatim parallels, but allusions or the expression of similar ideas." In tracing Syriac patristic quotations or specific agreements in Romanos, Petersen commits himself only to the "surest form of evidence for Romanos' acquaintance with and dependence upon the Syriac Ephrem," that is, "verbatim agreements."

Concerning the Ephremic *memra* on the Sinful Woman, Petersen claims to have identified two specific "agreements" between it and Romanos' *kontakion*. Both of these, "E-13" and "E-14" according to Petersen's numbering (1985b, 183–185), are found in the *kontakion*'s ninth strophe, the scene in which the Sinful Woman purchases the perfume.[14] The first "agreement":

Νευροῦται μὲν ἡ πιστὴ   τοῖς τοιούτοις ῥήμασι,
   ποιεῖται δὲ τὴν σπουδὴν   πρὸς τὴν τοῦ μύρου ὠνήν,
καὶ παραγίνεται   βοῶσα τῷ μυροπράτῃ·
   Δός μοι, εἰ ἔχεις,   ἐπάξιον μύρον τοῦ φίλου μου,

The faithful woman took courage at such words
and hastened to purchase the perfume.
She reached the place calling to the perfume-seller,
"Give me, if you have it, a perfume worthy of my lover."
   (Romanos 21.9.1–4)

ܡܥܠܬܐ ܕܗܒܐ ܥܠ ܥܨܪܗ ܘܫܩܠܬ ܫܛܝܦܬܐ ܒܐܝܕܗ
ܘܗܦܟܬ ܕܬܐܙܠ ܒܥܓܠ ܒܐܘܠܨܢܐ ܠܘܬ ܒܣܡܐ

She put the gold in her palm
and took the alabaster jar in her hand.
She turned to leave and made haste
in distress to the perfume-seller.
   (Ephrem 4.69–72)

The second:

Wehofer, Maas, and Bickersteth: for these so-called "probable" and "possible" Greek patristic sources of Romanos, see Schork 1957, 171.

[14] I have followed here, as Petersen does, Grosdidier de Matons 1964–1981, 2.13–43, for the text of Romanos and Beck 1970, 1.78–91, for the text of the Ephremic *memra*. All English translations of Romanos and Ephrem are my own unless otherwise noted.

μηδὲν περὶ τιμήματος· τί ἀμφιβάλλεις μοι;

"Let there be no debate [lit. "nothing"] about the price; why do you haggle with me?"[15] (Romanos 21.9.7)

ܗܡܢܐ ܚܢܢܐܝܬ ܠܐ ܒܥܐ ܐܢܐ ܘܐܦܠܐ ܠܡܬܦܠܓܘ ܠܐ ܚܢܐ [16]

"I do not seek your perfume free of charge, and I am not wanting to haggle over the price."
(Ephrem 4.119–120)

For each "agreement" Petersen makes only a few short comments. Concerning the first he notes that the idea of "making haste" appears in both passages and he remarks that "the development of the dialogue in the two writers is not identical, but the incident is the same" (1985b, 184). Regarding the second "agreement" Petersen points out that both poets use the negative in expressing the Sinful Woman's ability to pay: he parallels μηδὲν περὶ τιμήματος with ܠܐ ܚܢܐ. Petersen comments on the second "agreement" that "this is the sole direct parallel in the story which meets our criterion of a literal borrowing" (1985b, 185).

Following his collection of the twenty-one "agreements," including the two above, Petersen provides a summary of the results of his study in a short chapter titled "Conclusions Regarding Romanos and the Syriac Ephrem" (1985b, 195–197). His main purpose here seems to be to point out what he considers to be the incontestability of his findings. He emphasizes that he neglected to include "parallels which Romanos might have acquired from other sources." In contrast to such "echoes," as he calls them, the "agreements" that he found are "decisive" in proving that Romanos "used" Ephrem. He proceeds to enumerate also six "points of contact" between Romanos and Ephrem that he thinks are significant but not necessarily decisive like the "agreements." These common features include acrostics using the poets' own names, dialogues, hortatory beginnings, refrains, closing prayers of supplication and "the extensive use

---

[15] Maas and Trypanis, in their edition of Romanos' *kontakia*, print a different reading of 21.9.7 (Ox. 10.9.7): they prefer taking μηδὲν περὶ τιμήματος νῦν ἀμφιβάλῃς μοι: ("Don't be uncertain/doubtful [i.e. haggle] with me now concerning the price.") altogether as a negative imperative, which may have more resonance with the potential parallel in the Ephremic *memra*.

[16] I have removed the *seyame* that were mistakenly printed over ܚܢܐ (sic).

of oxymoron." Petersen ends this concluding chapter by claiming that he could have found "many more Ephremic parallels" in Romanos had he not committed himself to "literal agreements" and accepted in addition "similar ideas" or "expressions which approximate those of Romanos."

Robert Murray in his (otherwise positive) review of Petersen's book concludes with the devastating assertion that, of the twenty-one "agreements" that Petersen adduces, only the two quoted above and two others ("E-1" and "E-17") are probably legitimate (Murray 1989). Murray does not suggest criteria for his conclusion but remarks that "for most of the rest, and above all when both have an Old Testament passage in mind, I find the case interesting but not proven." He goes on to point to research on Genesis 22 by Brock that covers the "intervening writers" (that is, between Ephrem and Romanos) and "establish[es] the link between Ephrem and Romanos more surely than any other work yet published," including Petersen (Murray 1989, 260).[17] Perhaps Murray's most suggestive criticism of Petersen's enterprise, however, is the comment that "it is always possible that within a tradition different authors can independently express similar thoughts, either from knowledge of the same traditions, or because they share similar methods of meditation, reasoning, and poetic expression" (ibid).

Petersen's comments on the Sinful Woman poems and Murray's review of Petersen's book bring up two issues that are worthy of further investigation here. First, I would emphasize that Petersen only concerns himself with what he considers to be verbal parallels between the two texts and does not explore the implications of modifications in the narrative and dialogues introduced by Romanos. It is my contention that the original context of the material that has been adapted is important for determining how Romanos is using it: if it can be shown that the passage he is borrowing becomes more or less significant in his own *kontakion*, then it might be possible to suggest reasons—poetic, theological or otherwise—for the uniqueness of his appropriation. Second, the question of what constitutes a "borrowing" or an "agreement" is not addressed by either

---

[17] See, e.g., Brock 1981; 1986; 1989. Brock's work is central to the issue of the present argument not least because he suggests that Romanos appropriated material from fifth and sixth-century Syriac writings in his *kontakion* on the Sacrifice of Isaac: e.g., Brock 1989, 143–151, esp. 149. Romanos' *kontakion* on the Sacrifice of Isaac is SC 3 (Grosdidier de Matons 1964–1981, 1.129–165) and Ox. 41 (Maas and Trypanis 1963, 322–330).

Petersen or Murray, though both make confident judgments about what should be accepted or rejected. This entire debate partly rests on a problem of definitions. These definitions are worth considering more closely.

In order to consider the limits and method of Romanos' appropriation of an Ephremic text, it will be worthwhile at this point to examine the context of the material that Petersen claims Romanos used. From a thematic point of view, I suggest that Petersen's statement, quoted above, that "the development of the dialogue in the two writers is not identical" is probably more significant for the question of "borrowing" than he acknowledged.

The homily attributed to Ephrem devotes sixty-five lines to the dialogue between the Sinful Woman and the perfume-seller in his *memra* (69–134).[18] Here the perfume-seller is the dominant figure in the encounter, receiving the majority of the lines (77–112) and providing the catalyst for the revelation to the reader/audience of the Sinful Woman's conversion. She reveals to the perfume-seller, who draws out her confession with references to her former life, that her disheveled "appearance" (ܐܣܟܡܐ; line 79) and "fouled clothing" (ܠܒܘܫܐ; 89)— these words are repeated elsewhere as a code for the theme of repentance—are due to the fact that "the one who endures" (ܡܣܝܒܪܢܐ ܗܘ; 125) "stole [her] sins and debts" (ܗܘ ܓܢܒ ܚܘܒܝܗ ܘܚܛܗܝܗ; 131). Whereas in Romanos' hymn the poet himself indicates the Sinful Woman's repentance in the *prooimion* (21.pr. 2.2), in the Ephremic *memra* it is the dialogue with the perfume-seller that brings her conversion to the fore.[19]

Contrary to Ephrem's narrative, the perfume-seller plays a very minor role in Romanos, receiving only three lines of speech. He merely questions the Sinful Woman about the recipient of the perfume:

... "Λέξον μοι   τίς ἐστιν ὃν ἀγαπᾶς,
ὅτι τοσοῦτον σὲ   ἐπύρωσε πρὸς τὸ φίλτρον·
ἆρα κἂν ἔχει τι ἄξιον τούτου τοῦ μύρου μου;"

---

[18] The dialogue with the perfume-seller is especially significant because it appears first in the Ephremic *memra*. It entered Greek literature by the sixth century whether through the prose homily of Pseudo-Chrysostom (undated) or through Romanos. From its entry into the Greek tradition it makes its way through the Cyprus Passion Cycle into medieval Latin literature: see Mahr 1942.

[19] For the significance of the *prooimion* in Romanos' poetry, see Barkhuizen 1989; and 1990, 38–41.

... "Tell me who it is that you love,
since he has incited you so much for the love potion.
Can he really possess something worthy of my perfume?"
(21.10.2–4)

Following his question, the Sinful Woman proceeds over the next strophe and a half (21.10.7–21.11.11) to confess that the man whom she loves is "the Son of David...Son of God and God" and to compare herself to Michal who loved David just as she loves and desires "the one [descended] from David" (τὸν ἐκ Δαυίδ; 21.11.6). From there she takes the perfume and goes off to Simon's house, and the perfume-seller does not speak or appear again.

The perfume-seller scene is no doubt a significant connection between the two poets. It is remarkable, however, that Romanos has appropriated so little of the Ephremic version. The two "agreements" that Petersen suggests are, if legitimate, very minor appropriations. Concerning the first, the common use of "haste" is a tenuous strand with which to make a connection, especially given that the noun σπουδή occurs sixty-eight times in Romanos' *cantica genuina*, that is, almost once per poem.[20] The second "agreement," that of the Sinful Woman's unwillingness to haggle over the perfume's price, is the more plausible of the two, and it may ultimately prove to be an instance of verbal copying by Romanos.

Concerning the issue at hand, however—that of larger narrative or poetic appropriations by Romanos—I would suggest that only at two places, including the dialogue with the perfume-seller, can it be reasonably suggested that Romanos knew the Ephremic *memra*. First, Petersen rightly, I think, points to strophe 9 and the perfume-seller scene in Ephrem's *memra* as thematically the most significant for later Christian writers, and he notes that all previous studies of Romanos, except for the related work of Mahr on the Cyprus Passion Cycle, have missed this crucial connection to the Syriac tradition (1985b, 184).[21] But, as for the famous perfume-seller himself, his appearance is almost perfunctory for Romanos: it is the *perfume* and not the perfume-seller that takes a prominent role. In this vein, much more weight is placed by Romanos on the scene at Simon's house, which may be evidence of the influence of Jacob of Sarug (as argued above in the Introduction to the translation).

---

[20] This number is based on my own search of the *TLG*.
[21] See Mahr 1942, passim and Mahr 1947, 36–37.

Another possible example, omitted by Petersen, of Romanos appropriating a narrative element from the Ephremic *memra* is the common appearance at the end of the two poems of Christ's explanation of the parable of the two debtors. In Luke 7:36–50 Jesus does not explain that Simon is the greater debtor but only implies it by saying, "Therefore, I tell you, her sins, which were many, have been forgiven; hence she has shown great love. But the one to whom little is forgiven loves little" (7:47). However, in both the Ephremic homily and Romanos, Jesus takes pains to make sure that the point comes across: both poets have Jesus tell Simon directly that he is the debtor who owed more (Romanos 21.16; Ephrem 4.352–354).[22]

To contextualize these literary resonances, it is appropriate to consider what narrative elements Romanos clearly has not appropriated from the Ephremic *memra*. The most significant omission is that of the character of Satan, who has a prominent role both in the Ephremic *memra* as well as in the anonymous *soghitha* on the Sinful Woman (see below). The poem attributed to Ephrem emphasizes the psychological tension of the Sinful Woman's repentance by having Satan, disguised as one of her former lovers, meet her en route to Simon's house and try to persuade her to turn back to her former ways. He overheard her conversation with the perfume-seller, so he knows of her repentance (lines 133–156), but he must interrogate her to find out where she is taking the perfume. She survives his interrogation and defies his temptations, and he goes off sulking (225–233) while she proceeds to Simon's door. Leaving the Sinful Woman to weep and cry out to God for forgiveness outside Simon's house (277–294), Satan goes to Simon (inside his house?) and tries to tempt him not to receive the woman (262–273 and Beck 1970, 1. Appendix 1, 43–51). Simon also refuses Satan's temptation and, at least in this scene, comes off as a hero (Beck 1970, 1. Appendix 1, 1–42). None of this narrative, which is essential to the homily attributed to Ephrem, is present in Romanos' *kontakion*.

There are several other important elements of Ephrem's *memra* that Romanos leaves out of his *kontakion*, such as the motif of "Christ the Physician" (see above) and that of "the hidden and the revealed", but the

---

[22] Although Romanos has the superior debtor owing "50" and the inferior "5," the biblical text and the Ephremic *memra* both have "500" and "50" respectively. The biblical text, which has δηνάρια, is the only one of the three to specify a denomination.

absence of Satan is the most striking.²³ Overall, there seems to be very little that Romanos has taken directly from the Ephremic *memra* outside of the purchase of costly perfume.

IV. NOTE ON THE TEXT OF THE *SOGHITHA* ON THE SINFUL WOMAN AND SATAN

In the introduction to his text and translation of this *soghitha* on the Sinful Woman and Satan and of another medieval *soghitha* on the same theme, Brock outlines the manuscript tradition of the poems (1988, 23–30). In the preparation of his critical text he used ten manuscripts dating from the 8th/9th century to the 13th, none of which contains the entire *soghitha*.²⁴ A few of these manuscripts are lacking either all the odd numbered stanzas or the even ones because they were written for only one half of the choir. Brock chose manuscript C (9th cent.) as the basic text of his edition for two reasons: 1) it preserves more stanzas than any other manuscript; and 2) it appeared to him to have a better text for those stanzas in which it differed from the equally old manuscripts (A, 8th/9th cent.; and B, AD 893). In the apparatus to this edition Brock includes all the manuscript readings for the poem and translates them along with the main text.

Brock had prepared an earlier edition of this *soghitha* that was handwritten by the former bishop of the Syrian Orthodox Archdiocese of Central Europe, His Eminence Metropolitan Mor Julios Yeshu Çiçek (1942–2005), a respected Syriac calligrapher.²⁵ This text, published together with twenty-five other Syriac dialogue poems, was based on manuscripts A and B alone because C was unknown to Brock at the time (Brock 1982; see also 1984). So his 1988 revised text is based on a separate, better tradition.

In manuscripts A and C, the *soghitha* is attributed to "Mar Ya'qob", that is, Jacob of Sarug. Brock warns, however, that "in liturgical manuscripts attributions need to be treated with caution" (1988, 24). Jacob's verse homily on this motif obviously deals with the Sinful Woman in a very

---

[23] For these two motifs in Ephrem generally, see Brock 1992, 41 and Murray 1975, 199–203 (Christ the Physician); and Brock 1992, 27 (the hidden and the revealed).

[24] All of these manuscripts are contained in British and American libraries: for a list of the libraries and catalogue numbers, see Brock 1988, 23–24.

[25] A short biography of Mor Julios can be found in Gülcan and Palmer 1980; a brief history of the Syrian Orthodox Archdiocese of Central Europe can be found in Brock 1980.

different manner from this *soghitha*, concentrating, as mentioned above, on the interaction between the woman and Jesus at Simon's house, and ignoring the characters of the perfume-seller and Satan altogether. However, despite this dissimilarity between the two, Brock thinks that it is possible that both were written by Jacob. He lists a number of phrasal parallels between the two poems and suggests that "some literary connection does seem likely." The possibilities according to Brock are: 1) the *soghitha* is indeed by Jacob, 2) the author of the *soghitha* knew Jacob's verse homily, or 3) the *soghitha* precedes Jacob, who incorporated into his homily a few ideas that he took from the dialogue poem. Brock finds no way to adjudicate between these three options and thus leaves the question open (1988, 25).

V. ROMANOS AND THE *SOGHITHA* ON THE SINFUL WOMAN AND SATAN

In a paper delivered in 1989 at a symposium on Near Eastern dispute and dialogue literature, Brock set out a typology of the various types of dispute poem in Syriac.[26] He emphasized the connections of these poems to earlier Mesopotamian literature and traced the history of the Syriac dispute poem up to its present-day descendants. It may be useful here to consider Brock's findings in some detail before analyzing the possible literary connections with Romanos' *kontakia*.

Some fifty dispute and dialogue poems in Syriac survive, the earliest of which date from the fourth century AD.[27] These poems are part of a long history of dispute literature in Near Eastern languages, including Sumerian,

---

[26] Brock 1991 is a condensation of earlier work on dispute poems, their manuscript tradition, and their inclusion in the Syrian liturgies (e.g. 1983a; 1983b; 1984; 1988); it includes a very helpful Appendix of the editions and translations of these poems (1991, 116–119).

[27] According to Brock the formal difference between "dispute" and "dialogue" poems in Syriac is based mainly on the tenor of the dispute: whereas the earliest Syriac poems are, like their Mesopotamian predecessors, precedence disputes proper, in the later dialogue poems the idea of precedence has generally disappeared (1991, 114). As he notes, it is also the case that dialogue poems are debates between biblical characters whereas dispute poems often employ non-biblical personifications (the months, the letters of the alphabet, etc.): for these personifications, see Brock 1985a, Murray 1983, and Drijvers 1991.

Akkadian, Middle Persian, and Jewish Aramaic (Brock 1983a, 38).[28] The early examples in Syriac are all by Ephrem,[29] but the numerous fifth and sixth-century dialogue poems are mostly anonymous.[30] Several date to the eighth and ninth century or later and are datable by their inclusion of rhyme, a feature which was introduced into Syriac poetry following its first interactions with Arabic poetry (Brock 1991, 113). This long tradition is perpetuated by several twentieth-century dispute poems in modern Syriac, including a debate between a kettle and two boys (Brock 1991, 109 n. 2).

The fifth and sixth-century dispute poem typically comprises a dialogue between two disputants in alternating stanzas or couplets.[31] The normal meter is the isosyllabic 4x7 pattern, a form known as the *soghitha* (Brock 1991, 110).[32] The disputants are sometimes personifications, such as Death and Sheol, but biblical characters are more common in the Syriac literature.[33] The structure of the poems is simple: there is a hortatory introduction that sets the scene, then comes the main dispute that normally contains a double alphabetic acrostic, and finally there is a conclusion that typically includes a doxology in the last verse (Brock 1983, 36).[34] Since there are twenty-two letters in the Syriac alphabet, the inclusion of the double

---

[28] On the early development of dispute literature, see now Murray 1995, 158–172.

[29] On the dispute poems in Ephrem's corpus, see Murray 1983 and 1995, 172–180. The Ephremic *memra* examined above is not considered by scholars to be a dispute poem in the formal sense: Ephrem's dispute poems proper are all *madrashe*, the poetic form of which the *soghitha* is considered to be a sub-species—but contrary to the *madrasha*, the *soghitha* "contains narrative with dramatic though not necessarily adversative dialogue" (Murray 1995, 173).

[30] Some of these are attributed to famous poets such as Narsai and Jacob of Sarug; as noted above, the *soghitha* on the Sinful Woman and Satan is attributed to Jacob (Brock 1988, 24–25).

[31] The combination of two disputants and a judge is also found: see Brock 1983a, 36–39.

[32] The *soghitha* was sung and usually has both a melody (ܩܠܐ) and a refrain (ܥܘܢܝܬܐ); it should be emphasized that the *soghitha* is not restricted to dialogue or dispute poems, nor does it necessarily have an acrostic (Brock 1991, 110 n.4).

[33] Personifications were standard in the older Mesopotamian traditions: see Brock 1984, 32–33.

[34] The structure of Sumerian and Akkadian poems is more complicated but similar: see Murray 1995, 160.

acrostic means that each dialogue poem must be at least forty-four stanzas long, but the poems often extend to more than fifty stanzas because of the introduction and conclusion: the *soghitha* on the Sinful Woman and Satan has sixty stanzas. The verses of the central dispute section are short and often alternately mimic one another. Thus, for example, in the *soghitha* on the Sinful Woman and Satan:

> Satan: You are a harlot, if you only realized it,
> so why are you off to this chaste man [Jesus]?
> You are crazy, girl,
> and you've no idea what you are saying.
>
> Woman: I am a harlot, that I recognize,
> a harlot like Rahab, who ended up in the right:
> Joshua saved her,
> and Jesus will save me.
> (stanzas 25–26; trans. Brock 1991, 110–111)

The way in which the Sinful Woman's verses play off of and reverse Satan's is typical for the genre and occurs in almost every pair of couplets in the present *soghitha*.

The majority of the dialogue poems have survived only in Syriac liturgical manuscripts, the earliest of which date to the ninth century (Brock 1983, 39–40; 1984, 35–36). In the West Syrian tradition these poems were included in the manuscripts of the *Fenqitho*, the massive hymnary that is organized according to the liturgical year.[35] The group of poems that is best attested in these manuscripts is that of the Holy Week cycle, when the dialogues are sung as hymns in the night office. The *soghitha* on the Sinful Woman and Satan belongs to this group and is found in the readings for Thursday of Holy Week.[36] From the eleventh century onward, it was

---

[35] The manuscript tradition for the *Fenqitho* is marked by a "haphazard" method of scribal copying: it seems that scribes often replaced or deleted verses at their own discretion, sometimes leaving dialogues that are almost completely incoherent (Brock 1984, 38). For the early development of the *Fenqitho*, see Baumstark 1910a, 49–53, 61–68, and 77–84. The word ܦܢܩܝܬܐ (*fenqitha*, "writing tablet, book") comes from the Greek πινακίδιον ("writing tablet"), the diminutive of πίναξ.

[36] Contemporary printed editions of the *Fenqitho* retain little of the dialogue poems: only "a relic" remains of the *soghitha* on the Sinful Woman and Satan, which has been shifted to Tuesday of Holy Week (Brock 1988, 22 n.7); for the modern

common for the alternate verses of the dialogue poems to be copied out separately for antiphonal readings: thus one side of the choir recited the verses for Satan and the other recited those for the Sinful Woman. In several manuscripts only one side of the poem has survived (Brock 1984, 38–40).[37]

Unlike the poems attributed plausibly to an individual writer, precise dating is impossible for most of the anonymous dialogue poems. Those that are shared by the East and West Syrian ecclesiastical traditions probably date from the early fifth century, that is, before the Christological controversies, while those that survive in only one tradition or the other may well be late fifth or sixth-century compositions (Brock 1984, 35–36).[38] Although the genre probably continued well into the sixth century, a *terminus ante quem* for many poems can be established before the early seventh century because "they contain none of the 'learned' features that characterize most Syriac writing from the seventh century onwards," (ibid.).

As Brock has said repeatedly, it would be helpful for those studying the interactions of the Greek and Syriac poetic traditions during this period if more precise dates could be assigned to the dialogue poems (e.g. 1983, 40–41; 1984, 36–37). While he has attempted relative dating based upon shared themes, these attempts are made more difficult by the uncertain authorship of many of the Greek writings involved. For example, the likelihood that a Greek prose homily attributed to Proklos of Constantinople retains modified versions of two earlier Syriac dialogue poems is high but unprovable because the attribution to Proklos is in dispute.[39] If it could be shown that the homily was definitely later than

---

editions of the West and East Syrian liturgical books, see Baumstark 1958, 216–224; Brock 1983b, 74–78; and Brock 1996, 184–208.

[37] This is the case for a few manuscripts of the *soghitha* on the Sinful Woman and Satan: see above. A dialogue between Job and his wife, for example, survives only in this divided state (Brock 1991, 117).

[38] This was also the opinion of Baumstark (1910b, 537–538), cited by Brock; the fact that the *soghitha* on the Sinful Woman and Satan survives only in manuscripts from the West Syrian tradition suggests that it is a post-Chalcedonian composition: see above.

[39] [Proklos], *Homily* 6 on the Theotokos (*CPG* 5805). The Syriac dialogues in question are one between the Angel and Mary and another between Mary and Joseph: for the former, see Lamy 1882–1902, 2.589–604 (text and Latin trans.), and for English translations of both, see Brock 1994, 111–124.

Proklos—and therefore not authentic—then Syriac priority would be almost guaranteed because the early dialogue poems that are shared between the eastern and western traditions were probably written just when Proklos himself was writing.[40] But the most recent editor of Proklos' homilies, François Leroy, claims that this one, *Homily* 6 on the Theotokos, is authentic, thus complicating attempts to show Syriac priority (Leroy 1967, 292).[41] Despite Leroy's assertion, Brock points out that the editor's arguments have been questioned and that these shared dialogues strongly suggest the early influence of Syriac dispute poetry on Greek literature of the period (Brock 1984, 36).

In a paper delivered to the same 1989 symposium on Near Eastern dialogues mentioned above, Averil Cameron cautioned that, by looking for specific examples of influence between Greek and Syriac, scholars are, metaphorically speaking, missing the forest for the trees: what is needed now is a broader view that takes into account the historical circumstances that lay behind the construction of this "popular" dispute literature.[42] She has two caveats for the current tendency to promote Syriac priority: 1) dramatic dialogue occurs in fifth and sixth-century Greek homilies that are clearly not influenced by Syriac models; and 2) the prevalence of dispute in early Byzantine literature, Greek and Syriac, must be linked to the larger contexts of theological debate and imperial acclamation.

Her first caveat, that dialogue was an important function of Greek writing during this period quite apart from Syriac influence, has also been suggested by Pauline Allen and Cornelis Datema in their work on the sixth-century homilist Leontios of Constantinople.[43] Leontios uses many rhetorical figures that were common to Greek literature from classical times on, but he also includes dramatic monologues and dialogues similar to the ones which have been put forward as evidence of a Syriac background for Romanos and other writers. Allen and Datema, however, nowhere promote a Syriac background for Leontios. Rather, they emphasize that he blends

---

[40] Of these two Syriac dialogue poems, only the one between the Angel and Mary is shared by both traditions, and Brock admits that the other, between Joseph and Mary, is most likely later than the fifth century (1984, 36 n.4).

[41] For the debates over the authenticity of this homily, see *CPG* 5805.

[42] Cameron 1991b; the same sentiment is expressed by Murray (1995, 183–184). For the idea that homilies from this period are in some sense popular literature, see Averil Cameron 1991a, 96–101; and Cunningham 1995.

[43] Datema and Allen 1987, 44–48 and Allen and Datema 1991, 14–16.

the dialogues with traditional rhetorical figures so completely that it seems to them that he is fully within the Greek tradition (Allen and Datema 1991, 5).[44] Thus, on the basis of Leontios as well as earlier Greek homilists that used dialogue, like Amphilochios of Ikonion, Cameron argues that something more than simply "eastern influence" is needed to explain the rise of dialogue in early Byzantine homiletics (Cameron 1991b, 96).[45] In this regard she points to Greek political and ecclesiastical acclamation literature of the fifth through seventh centuries.

In 1912 Paul Maas, shortly after publishing the definitive article on the origins of the *kontakion* (Maas 1910), sought out the significance of these metrical acclamations for the early Byzantines (Maas 1912; see also Maas 1907 and 1962).[46] While no one, including Maas, has since attempted a detailed comparison of the acclamations and dramatic homilies, it would be remarkable given their similar structures if there was not an important connection between them. George La Piana long ago claimed that there had existed a "Byzantine Theater," a continuous dramatic tradition in the homilies of the Byzantine Church.[47] While it has been acknowledged by several others after La Piana that dramatic dialogue was somehow central to

---

[44] It certainly could be argued that this is not a basis for denying Syriac influence, especially considering the fact that Allen and Datema do play up the dialogic element of Leontios' sermons.

[45] Amphilochios does not, however, employ dialogue as often as Leontios. For the use of dialogue in Amphilochios, see van Rompay and Datema 1978; for the connections between Amphilochios, Romanos, and the Syriac traditions concerning the motif of the Sacrifice of Isaac (Gen 22), see Brock 1989, 143; and Glenthøj 1997, 261 n.33 and 263 n.42.

[46] The most recent comprehensive study of acclamations in this period (and earlier) is Roueché 1984, but Alan Cameron 1976 (Chapter 9 and Appendix C) and Mary Whitby and Michael Whitby 1989 (113–114) also discuss them.

[47] See La Piana 1912 and 1936; for more moderate approaches to the question of Byzantine religious drama, see Schork 1966 and Brock 1984, 37. The only known example of the Syriac dialogue poems being acted out is that of the Cherub and the Penitent Thief, which continues in some Iraqi mountain villages and was described by W.A. Wigram, one of the members of the Archbishop of Canterbury's Mission to the Church of the East (1929, 198; quoted with information about the manuscript tradition in Brock 1984, 47–48).

the "thought world" of early Byzantine writers,[48] Averil Cameron has asserted that the wide occurrence of dispute during this period may be "an attempt to find a new systemization of knowledge" (Averil Cameron 1991b, 100). This dispute-milieu—including dialogue poems, acclamations and dramatic homilies—is not yet fully analyzed and explained, and, as Cameron says, "to draw a line of contact [between these phenomena] may require an act of historical imagination," (Averil Cameron 1991b, 99), but the suggestion of influence nevertheless provides a possible historical framework for discussing dispute and dialogue in Syriac and Greek poetry during this period.

I suggested that the fifth and sixth-century Syriac poems might provide more substantial evidence of Romanos' appropriation of Syriac poetry because they were written closer to his lifetime, within this acclamation and debate atmosphere that Averil Cameron has described. I have tried to demonstrate this positively for Jacob of Sarug in my analysis above. However, while it is clear, as Brock has already shown, that the anonymous *soghitha* on the Sinful Woman and Satan knows and consciously alludes to the Ephremic *memra* on the Sinful Woman—and thus falls directly in line with the rest of the Syriac tradition—there seems to be no literary connection, as I will show below, between the *soghitha* and Romanos. All indications suggest that either he chose not to employ this poem or did not know it at all.

Unlike the Ephremic *memra* and Romanos' *kontakion*, the *soghitha* on the Sinful Woman and Satan does not deal directly with the biblical scene of Luke 7:36–50, although there are some signs that the *soghitha* takes its inspiration from that passage.[49] Instead, the *soghitha* features at its center a fictional conversation between the Sinful Woman and Satan that takes place subsequent to her purchase of the perfume but just before she goes off to

---

[48] E.g. MacCormack 1982, 298–302 and Allen and Datema 1991, 8–14. For the Byzantine reception of Romanos himself as a homiletical model, see Cunningham 2008.

[49] The anonymity of the woman and the mention of "Simon's house" (stanza 5) demonstrate that the author was following the Synoptic account (Brock 1988, 21 n. 4). Possible Lukan priority is shown only by the fact that she kisses Jesus' feet (stanza 60), which occurs only in Luke. On the other hand, there is no mention that Simon is a Pharisee, as he is in Luke but not Matthew or Mark ("Simon the Leper"), and at one point the woman claims to be intending to anoint Jesus' head, which occurs in Matthew, Mark, and John only.

Simon's house. There is a comparatively long nine-stanza introduction in which the poet relates that the "Compassionate Doctor" (ܐܣܝܐ ܘܡܪܚܡܢܐ) came to earth to "heal wounds" and to "cleanse the stains of the soul" (stanzas 2–3).[50] The Sinful Woman is introduced as one of several biblical characters that were "caught" (5) by the Doctor.[51] The dialogue follows, emphasizing her decision to repent: in his stanzas Satan presents arguments against such a decision and she refutes his arguments one by one. Brock, in his introduction to this text, suggests that the dialogic structure of this poem brings out the "inner psychological conflict through which the woman might be thought to have gone" (Brock 1988, 22). At the end of the dialogue there is a three-stanza conclusion in which the Sinful Woman "takes the unguent in the jar / and sets off lovingly to God," (stanza 58). The poem finishes with an invocatory doxology in which the Son of God is called upon by the poet to "forgive our sins too, just as you did her" because "you forgive your church / which consumes Your body and blood at the altar" (stanzas 59–60).

There are several indications that the author of this *soghitha* was aware of the homily attributed to Ephrem.[52] The most obvious of these is the appearance of Satan, who has a prominent, even dominating, role in both poems. In both poems Satan meets the woman at the same place on her journey: she has just bought the perfume but has not reached Simon's house yet. In the *soghitha*, however, Satan is not disguised, whereas in the *memra* he adopts the guise of one of her former lovers, never acknowledging his real identity. While the appearance of Satan as himself in the *soghitha* may seem more simplistic, it betrays the connection that the *soghyatha* have to the genre of the dispute poem in that it concentrates on the argument and not

---

[50] The use of the Christ as Physician motif at the beginning of the poem probably intentionally parallels the introduction of the Ephremic *memra*: compare especially the description of Christ in lines 5–12 of the latter.

[51] Included with the Sinful Woman, who comes at the end of the list, are the "blind", the "paralytic", the "lame", Zacchaeus, Zebedee's sons, and the Samaritan woman (stanzas 4–5); this list parallels that of the Ephremic poem, lines 5–6.

[52] At the end of his critical text Brock lists a number of parallels between this *soghitha*, the Ephremic *memra*, and Jacob of Sarug's *memra*, which he calls "small parallels in phraseology, cumulatively significant" (Brock 1988, 54); I have included most of these in my analysis of Jacob above.

the story.⁵³ As already mentioned, Satan never appears in Romanos' *kontakion* on the Sinful Woman or in Jacob of Sarug's *memra*. Yet, Allen has noted that Satan appears more frequently in sixth-century Greek homilists, including Romanos, than he does in the fifth-century (Allen 1998, 210). Consequently, the absence of Satan here is all the more striking in that context.

Another indication that the author of the *soghitha* knew the Ephremic *memra* is the reference to the purchase of the perfume in stanzas 48–49:

> Satan: Why did you go to the merchant of unguents [ܟܣܡܐ],
> what is that jar for?
> Have your lovers come to visit you?
> Are you wanting to have a fine time [ܠܟܣܡܝ]
> with them?
>
> Woman: I am off to God,
> and I am taking this jar with me
> To anoint that Head of life [ܐܙܡܥܐ ܘܪܡܫܐ]:
> he will then forgive my sins and I will come back.⁵⁴
> (stanzas 48–49; trans. Brock 1988, 50)

Although the perfume-seller scene is left out of the dialogue, this acknowledgement of its prior occurrence in the narrative is a conscious allusion to the Ephremic *memra*. Romanos, as mentioned previously, also treats the perfume-seller scene in a perfunctory manner, and, consequently, it might be suggested that this *soghitha* was Romanos' inspiration for doing so. It is obviously more likely, however, that the two poets made independent references to the perfume-seller since there are no other

---

⁵³ While the poem has its roots in the dispute literature (Brock 1988, 22), it cannot be said to contain the intense debating style that proper dispute poems have; also, there is no adjudication following the debate which is typical of the earlier dispute poems (Brock 1984, 32).

⁵⁴ It is very interesting that the Sinful Woman says here she wants to anoint the "Head"—even if only figuratively—since in Luke (7:38) the woman anoints Jesus' feet; in Matthew (26:7) and Mark (14:3) she anoints his head; in John (12:3) she anoints both head and feet. Although there are other indications, as noted above, that the author of the *soghitha* was possibly inspired by the Lukan text, this is an example in Syriac of the conflation of the Gospel stories that was common in the West but uncommon in the East: see Brock 1988, 21 n. 4 and Mahr 1942.

indications that Romanos used this *soghitha* and their use of the motif is different.

There are other minor connections between the *soghitha* and Ephrem worth noting. For example, they use similar bird imagery to describe the Sinful Woman and her escape from Satan's clutches. This is a passage from the *soghitha*:

Satan: My pretty dove [ܝܘܢܝ ܫܦܝܪܬܐ], what is up with you?
    Who has wheedled you so that you are rebelling
        against me?
    It is a long time since you have been living with me,
        and do you now take wing [ܡܦܪܚܬܝ ܟܢܦܐ], as I look on?

Woman: I am a guileless dove [ܝܘܢܐ ܐܢܐ ܐܡܨܥܬܐ],
    and I have escaped from your claws [ܛܦܪܝܟ]:
    Christ the eagle [ܢܫܪܐ] has rescued me
    and I live under his wings [ܟܢܦܘܗܝ].
    (stanzas 32–33; trans. Brock 1988, 48)

The homily attributed to Ephrem scatters similar imagery throughout. The author says in his introduction that the Sinful Woman directed her footsteps in the path of "the heavenly eagle" (ܢܫܪܐ ܫܡܝܢܐ; line 59), and later he has Satan wonder to himself how he will set a "bird trap" (ܦܚܐ; 234) for her. Towards the end of the *memra* the Sinful Woman tells Christ that she was a "sparrow" (ܨܦܪܐ) hunted by a "hawk" (ܢܨܐ) but she found shelter in his nest (288–289). Although the language is not the same, the imagery is very similar and probably shows that the author of the *soghitha* was drawing on the Ephremic *memra*'s vivid descriptions of the Sinful Woman's "flight" from her tempter. These examples are, of course, very similar to Jacob's appropriation of the same imagery from the Ephremic *memra*.

One further connection between these Syriac poems may be their descriptions of the Sinful Woman's seductive attire. In the Ephremic *memra* the poet tells in his introduction how as part of her repentance she washed the deadly "eye-black" (ܟܘܚܠܐ, 48) from her eyes and took off her alluring "bracelets" (ܩܠܒܐ, 50). The same and similar words are used by Satan in the *soghitha* when he reminds the Sinful Woman of her former life (stanzas 44 and 50). Taken altogether these parallels between the Ephremic *memra* and the anonymous *soghitha* suggest that the author of the latter was, just like

Jacob, probably well aware of the poem attributed to Ephrem and alluded to it in a number of ways.

In contrast to the use that the author of the *soghitha* made of Ephrem's *memra*, there seem to be few (if any) instances where Romanos appropriated material from the *soghitha*. In fact, it is doubtful whether he knew it at all. Had he known it there is still probably little genuine dialogue that Romanos could have taken from the poem once he decided not to include the character of Satan. In fact, in Romanos' poem the Sinful Woman has already repented and passed the stage of temptation at the very beginning: no tempting character is needed, be it the perfume-seller, a former lover, or Satan himself. Brock, however, has emphasized the "psychological", even "cinematographic," tension that is displayed in the Syriac poems (the Ephremic *memra* and the *soghitha*) through Satan's temptation of the Sinful Woman (Brock 1988, 22; 1991, 115); Romanos' poem obviously lacks that same tension due to the absence of any temptation scene.

Nevertheless, despite the fact that Romanos did not incorporate Satan into his poem, there are a few references to biblical women in the *soghitha* that Romanos could have made use of had he thought them appropriate. The only one of these women who does appear in Romanos, however, is Rahab, the prostitute who hid the Israelite spies in Jericho and subsequently received mercy for her brave act (Joshua 2 and 6). This is how Romanos connects her to the Sinful Woman in one of the latter's soliloquies:

Ἐδέξατο ἡ Ῥαὰβ κατασκόπους πρότερον
    καὶ τῆς δοχῆς τὸν μισθὸν ὡς πιστὴ εὗρε ζωήν·
τῆς γὰρ ζωῆς τύπος ὑπῆρχε τούτους ὁ πέμψας,
    τοῦ Ἰησοῦ μου βαστάζων τὸ τίμιον ὄνομα.
Σωφρονοῦντας τότε πόρνη ξενοδοχεῖ,
    νῦν παρθένον ἐκ παρθένου πόρνη ζητεῖ ἀλεῖψαι μύρῳ·
ἐκείνη μὲν ἀπέλυσεν οὕσπερ ἀπέκρυψεν·
    ἐγὼ δὲ ὃν ἠγάπησα μένω κατέχουσα,
οὐχ ὡς κατάσκοπον κλήρων, ἀλλ' ὡς ἐπίσκοπον πάντων
    κρατῶ, καὶ ἐξεγείρομαι ἐκ τῆς ὕλης
τοῦ βορβόρου τῶν ἔργων μου.

Once, the woman Rahab received [the Israelite] spies.
As a faithful woman she received life, the reward for her sheltering [them],
because [Joshua] the one who sent them, was a prototype of [true] life—
he ennobled the precious name of my Jesus.
Then a harlot welcomed temperate foreigners;

> now, [another] harlot seeks to anoint the Virgin Son of a Virgin with perfume.
> That woman [Rahab] set free those whom she had hidden;
> but I shall never let go of the one whom I desired.
> He is not a spy in a strange land; instead, he watches over all things.
> I shall grasp him and rise from the muck
> and the squalor of my deeds. (Romanos 21.7)

The *soghitha* refers to Rahab in a similar way, also playing on the names of Joshua and Jesus:[55]

> Woman: A prostitute I am, I do not deny it—
> a sister of Rahab who was put on the right path
> [lit. was justified];
> Jesus (Joshua) son of Nun saved her,
> Jesus our Lord will save me.
> (stanza 26; trans. Brock 1988, 47)

Although both poems include the obvious onomastic play on Jesus' Aramaic name, they employ Rahab differently. Romanos emphasizes what Rahab did for the spies, but the author of the *soghitha* focuses on what Joshua did for Rahab as a reward. The Sinful Woman in Romanos expects that Jesus, when she goes to him, will keep her for eternity just as Rahab kept the spies for a time; the Sinful Woman in the *soghitha* makes only the more obvious connection, allying herself with Rahab because they are both prostitutes hoping for deliverance. Thus, the Old Testament reference is the same in the two poems but its interpretation is quite different.

Romanos refers to other biblical women for whom the parallel with the Sinful Woman of Luke 7 is not quite as easily drawn: he has the Sinful Woman compare her weeping self to Hannah, who wept so much for her barrenness that Eli thought she was drunk (strophe 8), and Michal, who loved David as much as the Sinful Woman loves the Son of David (strophe 11). A recent translator of Romanos' *kontakia* remarks that such references "all testify to both the Melodist's skill at discovering such parallels and his congregation's ability to appreciate their inter-testamental relevance" (Schork 1995, 77). Quite apart from the question of Romanos' congregation's ability to grasp his biblical references (cf. Koder 1994; 1997–

---

[55] The Greek text does not include the word "Joshua" in line 3, but the inclusion of "name" (ὄνομα) in line 4 makes it clear that Romanos is playing on their names: see Grosdidier de Matons 1964–1981, 2.28.

1999; Hunger 1984), it seems to me that the poet's obvious knack for coming up with creative biblical parallels in his *kontakia* makes it all the more unlikely that he took this reference to Rahab from the *soghitha*. This was his natural creativity at work.

There are no other real points of comparison between these two poems, and thus it would appear that Romanos did not appropriate anything from the anonymous *soghitha* on the Sinful Woman and Satan. It should be emphasized, however, that the author of the *soghitha* seems to allude to the Ephremic *memra* on a number of occasions particularly in their shared accentuation of the (extra-biblical) role of Satan.[56] In this regard at least neither Romanos nor Jacob appropriates the tradition any more than they appropriate the *soghitha* itself: not only does neither poet include the character of Satan in his poem, but both concentrate more on the meeting of the Sinful Woman and Jesus. This is, in fact, a narrative element which both the Ephremic *memra* and the *soghitha* minimize in their treatments.

If any connection is to be made between Romanos and the *soghitha* it must be an indirect one. Averil Cameron's concerns about trying to identify specific borrowings have been noted, and her suggestion of a common, unspecific dispute culture is strengthened in this case because of the lack of a clear literary relationship: besides the biblical scene, the most significant element shared between the poems is of course dialogue itself. Romanos' *kontakion* retains less of the dispute-element and could justifiably be placed more comfortably within the framework of fifth- and sixth-century Greek homilists, with their heightened use of dramatic dialogue. On the other side of this genre spectrum, the anonymous *soghitha* reveals its Near Eastern roots as much by its form as by its treatment of this theme.

VI. Conclusion

Given some of the emphatic pronouncements about Romanos' dependence on Syriac sources for his *kontakia*, it is very significant to be able to show two cases where *he did not* clearly use a Syriac text that could well have been available to him. Schork, despite his insistence on Romanos' use of the Greek patristic tradition, when speaking of Syriac dramatic homilies, says, "Any investigation into the literary sources used by the Melodist reveals his

---

[56] This *soghitha* is alluded to in a medieval *soghitha* on this theme that develops Satan's character in a similar way and also makes use of Ephrem, though possibly through the earlier *soghitha:* see Brock 1988, 55–62.

debt to such works," (1966, 274). This study has shown that Schork's assertion is not always true: neither Ephrem's *memra* nor the *soghitha* on the Sinful Woman and Satan revealed any significant literary "debt" of Romanos. It could of course be an issue of chronology: the *soghitha* may easily postdate Romanos altogether, since Brock has placed it broadly "from the fifth to seventh centuries" on stylistic grounds (Brock 1988, 25). Yet a later dating of the *soghitha* does not, of course, prove that Romanos did not make use of the Syriac tradition. Generally speaking, it seems obvious that he was aware of the tradition and made use of it at times. However, I hope to have demonstrated that such borrowings need to be contextualized. All of these poems deserve to be read on their own terms, and the "borrowing" of one from another is likely to be indirect or unpredictable. In the case of the *kontakion* on the Sinful Woman, it is unexpected and exciting to be able to say that the argument for Romanos' use of the Ephremic *memra* and the *soghitha* is weaker than for Romanos' engagement with his near-contemporary Jacob of Sarug. The former Syriac poems had the weight of the Ephrem's authoritative name and the established genre of dispute behind them. While Jacob and Romanos' treatments are very different in some ways, the parallels between them prove to be stronger and more sophisticated than between each of them and any other poems.

ABBREVIATIONS

CPG   Geerard, M., et al., eds. 1974–2003. *Clavis Patrum Graecorum*. 5 vols. Turnhout: Brepols.

CSCO   Corpus Scriptorum Christianorum Orientalium

GEDSH   Brock, S.P., et al., eds. 2011. *The Gorgias Encyclopedic Dictionary of the Syriac Heritage*. Piscataway, NJ: Gorgias Press.

Ox.   Maas, P., and C. A. Trypanis, eds. 1963. *Sancti Romani Melodi Cantica: Cantica Genuina*. Oxford: Clarendon Press.

SC   Grosdidier de Matons, José, ed. 1964–1981. *Romanos le mélode: Hymnes*. 5 vols. Sources chrétiennes. Paris: Éditions du Cerf.

Works Cited

'Abd al-Masih, Y., ed. 1958–1960. "A Discourse by St. John Chrysostom on the Sinful Woman in the Saʿidic Dialect." *Bulletin de la société d'archéologie copte* 15: 11–39.
Albert, M., ed. 1976–1977. "Homélies contre les Juifs par Jacques de Saroug." *Patrologia Orientalis* 38: 3–242.
Allen, Pauline. 1998. "The Sixth-Century Greek Homily: A Re-Assessment". In *Preacher and Audience: Studies in Early Christian and Byzantine Homiletics*, ed. Mary B. Cunningham and Pauline Allen, 201–226. Leiden: Brill.
Allen, Pauline, and Cornelis Datema. 1991. *Leontius, Presbyter of Constantinople: Fourteen Homilies*. Byzantina Australiensia 9. Brisbane: Australian Association for Byzantine Studies.
Alwan, P. Khalil. 1986. "Bibliographie générale raisonée de Jacques de Saroug." *Parole de l'orient* 13: 313–384.
Amar, J.P., ed. 1995. *A Metrical Homily on Holy Mar Ephrem by Mar Jacob of Sarug*. Patrologia Orientalis 47/209. Turnhout: Brepols.
Ashbrook Harvey, S. 1990. "Jacob of Serug: Homily on Simeon the Stylite." In *Ascetic Behavior in Greco-Roman Antiquity: A Sourcebook*, 15–28. Minneapolis: Fortress Press.
———. 1998. "St. Ephrem on the Scent of Salvation." *Journal of Theological Studies* n.s. 49: 109–128.
———. 2001a. "2000 NAPS Presidential Address. Spoken Words, Voiced Silence: Biblical Women in Syriac Tradition." *Journal of Early Christian Studies* 9: 105–131.
———. 2001b. "Why the Perfume Mattered: The Sinful Woman in Syriac Exegetical Tradition." In *In Dominico Eloquio / In Lordly Eloquence: Essays on Patristic Exegesis in Honor of Robert Louis Wilken*, ed. P.M. Blowers et al., 69–89. Grand Rapids, MI: Eerdmans.

———. 2006. *Scenting Salvation: Ancient Christianity and the Olfactory Imagination*. Transformation of the Classical Tradition 42. Berkeley: University of California Press.

Ashbrook Harvey and Ophir Münz-Manor. 2010. *Jacob of Sarug's Homily on Jephthah's Daughter*. Metrical Homilies of Mar Jacob of Sarug 16. Piscataway, NJ: Gorgias Press.

Baldwin, Barry. 1991. "Romanos the Melode." In *The Oxford Dictionary of Byzantium*, ed. A.P. Kazhdan, 3.1807–1808. Oxford: Oxford University Press.

Barkhuizen, G.W. 1989. "Romanos Melodos and the Composition of His Hymns: *Prooimion* and Final Strophe." *Hellenika* 40: 62–77.

———. 1990. "Romanos Melodos 10 (Oxf.): On the Sinful Woman."*Acta Classica* 33: 33–52.

Baumstark, Anton. 1910a. *Festbrevier und Kirchenjahr der syrischen Jakobiten: Eine liturgiegeschichtliche Vorarbeit*. Paderborn: F. Schöningh.

———. 1910b. Review of Paul Maas, *Frühbyzantinische Kirchenpoesie: I. Anonyme Hymnen des V–VI Jahrhunderts* (Bonn, 1910). *Byzantinische Zeitschrift* 19: 535–538.

———. 1922. *Geschichte der syrischen Literatur: Mit Ausschluss der christlich-palästinensischen Texte*. Bonn: A. Marcus und E. Webers.

———. 1958. *Comparative Liturgy*. Trans. F.L. Cross. London: A.R. Mowbray.

Beck, E. 1960. "Éphrem le syrien." In *Dictionnaire de spiritualité: Ascétique et mystique, doctrine et histoire*, 4.787–800. Paris: Éditions Beauchesne.

———. 1962. "Ephrem Syrus." In *Reallexikon für Antike und Christentum*, 5.520–531. Stuttgart: A. Hiersemann.

———, ed. 1966. *Des heiligen Ephraem des Syrers, Sermo de Domino Nostro*. 2 vols. CSCO 270–271, Scriptores Syri 116–117. Leuven: CSCO.

———, ed. 1970. *Des heiligen Ephrem des Syrers, Sermones II*. 2 vols. CSCO 311–312, Scriptores Syri 134–135. Leuven: CSCO.

Bedjan, Paul, ed. 1905–1910. *Homiliae Selectae Mar-Jacobi Sarugensis*. 5 vols. Paris and Leipzig: Via Dicta and Otto Harrassowitz.

Blum, J.G. 1983. "Zum Bau von Abschnitten in *Memre* von Jakob von Sarug." In *III Symposium Syriacum, 1980: Les Contacts du monde syriaque avec les autres cultures (Goslar, 7–11 septembre)*, ed. René Lavenant, 307–321. Orientalia Christiana Analecta 221. Rome: Pontifical Oriental Institute.

Bou Mansour, T. 1993. *La théologie de Jacques de Saroug*. Kaslik: Université Saint Esprit.

Bovon, François. 2002. *Luke 1: A Commentary on the Gospel of Luke 1:1–9:50*. Trans. Christine M. Thomas. Hermeneia. Minneapolis: Fortress Press.

Brière, Maurice, ed. 1948. "Les *Homilies Cathedrales* de Sévère d'Antioch: *Hom.* 118." *Patrologia Orientalis* 26: 357–374.

Brock, Sebastian P. 1978. "Baptismal Themes in the Writings of Jacob of Serugh." In *II Symposium Syriacum, 1976: Célébré du 13 au 17 septembre 1976 au Centre culturel Les Fontaines de Chantilly, France; Communications*, 325–347. Orientalia Christiana Analecta 205. Rome: Pontifical Institute of Oriental Studies.

———. 1979. *The Holy Spirit in the Syrian Baptismal Tradition*. Poona: Anita Printers.

———. 1980. "Syrian Orthodox Church in Europe." *Sobornost* 2: 66–67.

———. 1981. "An Anonymous Syriac Homily on Abraham (Gen. 22)." *Orientalia Lovainensia Periodica* 12: 226–260.

———, ed. 1982. *Sogyatha Mgabbyata*. Holland: Monastery of Ephrem the Syrian.

———. 1983a. "Dialogue Hymns of the Syriac Churches." *Sobornost* 5: 35–45.

———. 1983b. "Mary and the Gardener: An East Syrian Dialogue *Soghitha* for the Resurrection." *Parole de l'orient* 11: 223–234.

———. 1984. "Syriac Dialogue Poems: Marginalia to a Recent Edition." *Le Muséon* 97: 29–58.

———. 1985a. "A Dispute of the Months and Some Related Syriac Texts." *Journal of Semitic Studies* 30: 181–211.

———. 1985b. "Syriac and Greek Hymnography: Problems of Origin." *Studia Patristica* 16: 77–81.

———. 1986. "Two Syriac Verse Homilies on the Binding of Isaac." *Le Muséon* 99: 61–129.

———. 1987a. "Dramatic Dialogue Poems." In *IV Symposium Syriacum, 1984: Literary Genres in Syriac Literature (Groningen-Oosterhesselen, 10–12 September)*, ed. H.J.W. Drijvers, 135–147. Orientalia Christiana Analecta 229. Rome: Pontifical Institute for Oriental Studies.

———. 1987b. "The Published Verse Homilies of Isaac of Antioch, Jacob of Serugh, and Narsai: Index of Incipits." *Journal of Semitic Studies* 32: 279–313.

———. 1988. "The Sinful Woman and Satan: Two Syriac Dialogue Poems." *Oriens Christianus* 72: 21–62.

———. 1989. "From Ephrem to Romanos." *Studia Patristica* 20: 139–151.

———. 1991. "Syriac Dispute Poems: The Various Types." In *Dispute Poems and Dialogues in the Ancient and Medieval Near East: Forms and Types of Literary Debates in Semitic and Related Literatures*, ed. G.J. Reinink and H.L.J. Vantisphout, 109–119. Leuven: Peeters.

———. 1992. *The Luminous Eye: The Spiritual World Vision of Saint Ephrem*. Kalamazoo, MI: Cistercian Publications.

———. 1994. *Bride of Light: Hymns on Mary from the Syriac Churches*. Kottayam: St. Ephrem Ecumenical Research Institute.

———. 1996. *Syriac Studies: A Classified Bibliography (1960–1990)*. Kaslik: Université Saint-Esprit.

———. 1997. *A Brief Outline of Syriac Literature*. Kottayam: St. Ephrem Ecumenical Research Institute.

———. 1998. "Syriac Studies: A Classified Bibliography (1990–1995)." *Parole de l'orient* 23: 241–350.

———. 2004. "Syriac Studies: A Classified Bibliography (1996–2000)." *Parole de l'orient* 29: 263–410.

———. 2009. *Jacob of Sarug's Homily on the Veil on Moses' Face*. Metrical Homilies of Mar Jacob of Sarug 1. Piscataway, NJ: Gorgias Press.

Brockelmann, Carl. 1928. *Lexicon Syriacum*. 2nd ed. Halle an der Saale: M. Niemeyer.

Cameron, Alan D.E. 1976. *Circus Factions: Blues and Greens at Rome and Byzantium*. Oxford: Clarendon Press.

Cameron, Averil M. 1991a. *Christianity and the Rhetoric of Empire: The Development of Christian Discourse*. Sather Classical Lectures. Berkeley and Los Angeles: University of California Press.

———. 1991b. "Disputations, Polemical Literature, and the Formation of Opinion in the Early Byzantine Period." In *Dispute Poems and Dialogues in the Ancient and Medieval Near East: Forms and Types of Literary Debates in Semitic and Related Literatures*, ed. G.J. Reinink and H.L.J. Vantisphout, 91–108. Leuven: Peeters.

Carpenter, Marjorie. 1970–1972. *Kontakia of Romanos, Byzantine Melodist*. 2 vols. Columbia, MO: University of Missouri Press.

Cross, F.L., and E.A. Livingstone, eds. 1997. *The Oxford Dictionary of the Christian Church*. 3rd ed. Oxford: Oxford University Press.

Cunningham, Mary B. 1995. "Innovation or Mimesis in Byzantine Sermons?" In *Originality in Byzantine Literature, Art, and Music: A Collection of Essays*, ed. A.R. Littlewood, 67–80. Oxford: Oxbow Books.

———. 2008. "The Reception of Romanos in Middle Byzantine Homiletics and Hymnography." *Dumbarton Oaks Papers* 62: 251–260.

Datema, Cornelis, and Pauline Allen, eds. 1987. *Leontii Presbyteri Constantinopolitani Homiliae*. Corpus Christianorum Series Graeca. Turnhout: Brepols.

Draguet, R. 1977. "Une méthode d'édition des textes syriaques." In *A Tribute to Arthur Vööbus: Studies in Early Christian Literature and Its Environment, Primarily in the Syrian East*, ed. R.H. Fischer, 13–18. Chicago: Lutheran School of Theology at Chicago.

Drijvers, H.J.W. 1991. "Body and Soul: A Perennial Problem." In *Dispute Poems and Dialogues in the Ancient and Medieval Near East: Forms and Types of Literary Debates in Semitic and Related Literatures*, ed. G.J. Reinink and H.L.J. Vantisphout, 122–134. Leuven: Peeters.

Elliott, J.K. 1974. "The Anointing of Jesus." *The Expository Times* 85: 105–107.

Field, F., ed. 1839. *Sancti patris nostri Joannis Chrysostomi Archiepiscopi Constantinopolitani homiliae in Matthaeum: Textum ad fidem codicum Mss. et versionum emendavit praecipuam lectionis varietatem adscripsit adnotationibus ubi opus erat et novis indicibus instruxit*. 3 vols. Cambridge: Cambridge University Press.

Frank, Georgia. 2006. "Romanos and the Night Vigil in the Sixth Century." In *Byzantine Christianity*, ed. Derek Krueger, 59–78. A People's History of Christianity 3. Minneapolis: Fortress Press.

Glenthøj, Johannes Bartholdy. 1997. *Cain and Abel in Syriac and Greek Writers (4th–6th Centuries)*. CSCO 567, Subsidia 95. Leuven: Peeters.

Graffin, F. 1974. "Jacques de Saroug." In *Dictionnaire de spiritualité: Ascétique et mystique, doctrine et histoire*, 8.56–60. Paris: Éditions Beauchesne.

———, ed. 1984. "Homélies anonymes du VIe siècle: Dissertation sur le Grand-Prêtre, homélies sur la pécheresse 1, 2, 3." *Patrologia Orientalis* 41.4/189: 389–534.

Graffin, F., and M. Albert. 2004. *Les lettres de Jacques de Saroug*. Patrimoine syriaque 3. Kaslik, Lebanon: Parole de l'orient.

Griffith, S.H. 1997. "'Faith Adoring the Mystery': Reading the Bible with St. Ephraem the Syrian." Père Marquette Lecture. Milwaukee, WI: Marquette University Press.

Grosdidier de Matons, José, ed. 1964–1981. *Romanos le mélode: Hymnes*. 5 vols. Sources chrétiennes. Paris: Éditions du Cerf.

———. 1977. *Romanos le mélode et les origines de la poésie religieuse à Byzance*. Paris: Éditions Beauchesne.

———. 1980. "Liturgie et hymnographie: *Kontakion* et *canon*." *Dumbarton Oaks Papers* 34/35: 31–43.

Gülcan, Isa, and Andrew Palmer. 1980. "The Syrian Orthodox Metropolitan of Central Europe." *Sobornost* 2: 68–71.

Halleux, A. de. 1978. "Hellénisme et syrianité de Romanos le mélode." *Revue d'histoire ecclésiastique* 73: 632–641.

Hansbury, Mary. 1998. *On the Mother of God*. Crestwood, NY: St. Vladimir's Seminary Press.
Haskins, Susan. 1993. *Mary Magdalen: Myth and Metaphor*. London: Harper Collins.
Hemmerdinger-Iliadou, D., and J. Kirchmeyer. 1960. "Éphrem (les versions)." In *Dictionnaire de spiritualité: Ascétique et mystique, doctrine et histoire*, 4.800–822. Paris: Éditions Beauchesne.
Hunger, H. 1984. "Romanos Melodos, Dichter, Prediger, Rhetor – und sein Publikum." *Jahrbuch der Österreichischen Byzantinistik* 34: 15–42.
Hunt, Hannah M. 1998. "The Tears of a Sinful Woman: A Theology of Redemption in the Homilies of St. Ephraim and His Followers." *Hugoye: Journal of Syriac Studies* 1.
———. 2004. *Joy-Bearing Grief: Tears of Contrition in the Writings of the Early Syrian and Byzantine Fathers*. The Medieval Mediterranean 57. Leiden: Brill.
———. 2010. "Sexuality and Penitence in Syriac Commentaries on Luke's Sinful Woman." *Studia Patristica* 45: 195–199.
Johnson, Scott Fitzgerald. 2002. "The Sinful Woman: A *Memra* by Jacob of Serugh." *Sobornost / Eastern Churches Review* 24: 56–88.
Kiraz, George Anton, ed. 2010. *Jacob of Serugh and His Times: Studies in Sixth-Century Syriac Christianity*. Gorgias Eastern Christian Studies 8. Piscataway, NJ: Gorgias Press.
Koder, J. 1994. "Justinians Seig über Salomen." In Θυμίασμα, στη μνήμη της Λασκαρίνας Μπούρα, 135–142. 2 vols. Athens: Benaki Museum.
———. 1997–1999. "Romanos Melodos und sein Publikum: Überlegungen zur Beeinflussung des kirklichen Auditoriums durch das Kontakion." *Anzeiger der philos.-histor. Klasse* 134: 63–69.
———. 2005. *Romanos: Die Hymnen*. 2 vols. Bibliothek der griechischen Literatur 62, 64. Stuttgart: Hiersemann.
———. 2008. "Imperial Propaganda in the Kontakia of Romanos the Melode." *Dumbarton Oaks Papers* 62: 275–291.
Kollamparampil, T. 1997. *Jacob of Serugh: Select Festal Homilies*. Rome: Center for Indian and Inter-Religious Studies.
———. 2010. *Salvation in Christ According to Jacob of Serugh: An Exegetico-Theological Study on the Homilies of Jacob of Serugh on the Feasts of Our Lord*. Gorgias Dissertations in Early Christian Studies 49. Piscataway, NJ: Gorgias Press.
Krueger, K. 2004. *Writing and Holiness: The Practice of Authorship in the Early Christian East*. Philadelphia: University of Pennsylvania Press.

———. 2006. "Romanos the Melodist and the Christian Self in Early Byzantium." In *Proceedings of the 21st International Congress of Byzantine Studies, London, 2006, vol. 1, Plenary Papers,* ed. Elizabeth Jeffreys, 247–266. Aldershot: Ashgate.
Krumbacher, Karl. 1907. *Miscellen zu Romanos.* Munich: K. B. Akademie der Wissenschaften.
Lamy, T.J., ed. 1882–1902. *Sancti Ephraem Syri, Hymni et Sermones.* 4 vols. Mechelen: H. Dessain.
La Piana, George. 1912. *Le rappresentazioni sacre nella letteratura bizantina dalle origini al secolo IX, con rapporti al teatro sacro d'occidente.* Grottaferrata: "S. Nilo".
———. 1936. "The Byzantine Theater." *Speculum* 11: 171–211.
Lash, Ephrem. 1995. *On the Life of Christ : Kontakia by Romanos the Melodist.* Sacred Literature Series. San Francisco: HarperCollins.
Legault, André. 1954. "An Application of the Form-Critique Method to the Anointings in Galilee (Lk 7, 36–50) and Bethany (Mt 26, 6–13; Mk 14, 3–9; Jn 12, 1–8)." *Catholic Biblical Quarterly* 16: 131–145.
Leloir, L., ed. 1963. *Saint Éphrem: Commentaire de l'Évangile concordant, texte syriaque (manuscrit Chester Beatty 709).* Chester Beatty Monographs. Dublin: Hodges Figgis.
Leroy, François Joseph, ed. 1967. *L'Homilétique de Proclus de Constantinople: Tradition manuscrite, inédits, études conexes.* Studi e Testi 247. Biblioteca Apostolica Vaticana: Vatican City.
Lienhard, J.T. 1994. *Origen: Homilies on Luke, Fragments on Luke.* Fathers of the Church 94. Washington, DC: Catholic University of America Press.
Maisano, Riccardo, ed. 2002. *Romano il melodo: Cantici.* 2 vols. Torino:Unione tipografico-editrice torinese.
———. 2008. "Romanos's Use of Greek Patristic Sources." *Dumbarton Oaks Papers* 62: 261–273.
Maas, P. 1906. "Die Chronologie der Hymnen des Romanos." *Byzantinische Zeitschrift* 15: 1–43.
———. 1907. "Grammatische und metrische Umarbeitungen in der Überlieferung des Romanos." *Byzantinische Zeitschrift* 16: 565–587.
———. 1910. "Das Kontakion." *Byzantinische Zeitschrift* 19: 285–306.
———. 1912. "Metrische Akklamationen der Byzantiner." *Byzantinische Zeitschrift* 21: 28–51.
———. 1962. *Greek Metre.* Trans. H. Lloyd-Jones. Oxford: Clarendon.
Maas, Paul, and C. A. Trypanis, eds. 1963. *Sancti Romani Melodi Cantica: Cantica Genuina.* Oxford: Clarendon Press.

———, eds. 1970. *Sancti Romani Melodi Cantica: Cantica Dubia*. Berlin: de Gruyter.

MacCormack, Sabine. 1981. *Art and Ceremony in Late Antiquity*. Transformation of the Classical Heritage 1. Berkeley: University of California Press.

Mahr, A.C. 1942. *Relations of Passion Plays to St. Ephrem the Syrian*. Columbus, Ohio: Wartburg Press.

———. 1947. *The Cyprus Passion Cycle*. Notre Dame: University of Notre Dame Press.

Martin, J.-P.P. 1876. "Lettres de Jacques de Saroug aux moines du couvent de Mar Bassus et à Paul d'Edesse." *Zeitschrift der deutschen morgenländischen Gesellschaft* 29: 217–275.

Mathews, E.G., J.P. Amar, and K. McVey. 1994. *St. Ephrem the Syrian, Selected Prose Works: Commentary on Genesis, Commentary on Exodus, Homily on Our Lord, Letter to Publius*. Fathers of the Church 91. Washington, DC: Catholic University of America Press.

McCarthy, Carmel. 1993. *Saint Ephrem's Commentary on Tatian's Diatessaron: An English Translation of Chester Beatty Syriac MS 709*. Oxford: Oxford University Press on behalf of the University of Manchester.

McCollum, Adam Carter. 2009. *Jacob of Sarug's Homily on Simon Peter, When Our Lord Said, "Get Behind Me, Satan."* Metrical Homilies of Mar Jacob of Sarug 22. Piscataway, NJ: Gorgias Press.

McVey, K.E. 1989. *Ephrem the Syrian: Hymns*. Classics of Western Spirituality. New York: Paulist Press.

Melki, J. 1983. "Saint Éphrem: Bilan de l'édition critique." *Parole de l'orient* 11: 3–88.

Murray, Robert M. 1975. *Symbols of Church and Kingdom: A Study in Early Syriac Tradition*. Cambridge: Cambridge University Press.

———. 1983. "St. Ephrem's Dialogue of Reason and Love."*Sobornost* 5: 26–40.

———. 1989. Review of Petersen 1985b. *Journal of Theological Studies* n.s. 40: 258–260.

———. 1995. "Aramaic and Syriac Dispute-Poems and Their Connections." In *Studia Aramaica: New Sources and New Approaches*, ed. M.J. Geller, et al., 157–187. Oxford: Oxford University Press.

Olinder, G. 1937. *Iacobi Sarugensis epistulae quotquot supersunt*. CSCO 110, Scriptores Syri 2.45. CSCO: Paris.

———. 1939. *The Letters of Jacob of Sarug: Comments on an Edition*. Lund-Leipzig: C.W.K. Gleerup and O. Harrassowitz.

Papoutsakis, Manolis. 2007. "The Making of a Syriac Fable: From Ephrem to Romanos." *Le Muséon* 120: 29–75.
Petersen, William L. 1985a. "The Dependence of Romanos the Melodist upon the Syriac Ephrem: Its Importance for the Origin of the *Kontakion*." *Vigiliae Christianae* 39: 171–187.
———. 1985b. *The Diatessaron and Ephrem Syrus as Sources of Romanos the Melodist*. Leuven: Peeters.
Pierre, M.-J. 1988. *Aphraate le sage persan: Les Exposés*. Sources chrétiennes. Paris: Du Cerf.
Prevost, G. 1843–1851. *The Homilies of S. John Chrysostom, Archbishop of Constantinople on the Gospel of Matthew*. 3 vols. J.H. Parker: Oxford.
Rilliet, F., ed. 1986. "Jacques de Saroug: Six homélies festales en prose." *Patrologia Orientalis* 43: 513–663.
———. 1993. "Une victime du tournant des études syriaques à la fin du XIXe siècle: Retrospective sur Jacques de Saroug dans la science occidentale." *ARAM* 5: 465–480.
———. 1994. "Jakob von Sarug." In *Reallexikon für Antike und Christentum*, 16.1217–1227. Stuttgart: A. Hiersemann.
Roueché, Charlotte. 1984. "Acclamations in the Later Roman Empire: New Evidence from Aphrodisias."*Journal of Roman Studies* 74: 181–199.
Rompay, L. van. 1993. "Romanos le Mélode: Un poète syrien à Constantinople." In *Early Christian Poetry: A Collection of Essays*, ed. J. den Boeft and A. Hilhorst, 283–296. Leiden: Brill.
Rompay, L. van, and Cornelius Datema, eds. 1978. *Amphilochii Iconiensis Opera*. Corpus Christianorum Series Graeca. Turnhout: Brepols.
Sauget, J.-M. 1974. Review of Vööbus 1973–1980, vols. 1–2. *Le Muséon* 77: 295–302.
———. 1975–1976. "Une homélie syriaque sur la pécheresse attribuée a un Évêque Jean." *Parole de l'orient* 6–7: 159–194.
Schork, R.J. 1957. *The Biblical and Patristic Sources of Christological Kontakia of Romanos the Melodist*. D.Phil. thesis, Oxford University.
———. 1960. "The Medical Motif in the *Kontakia* of Romanos the Melodist." *Traditio* 16: 353–363.
———. 1962. "Typology in the *Kontakia* of Romanos." *Studia Patristica* 6: 211–220.
———. 1966. "Dramatic Dimension in Byzantine Hymns." *Studia Patristica* 8: 271–279.
———. 1995. *Sacred Song from the Byzantine Pulpit: Romanos the Melodist*. Gainesville: University Press of Florida.

Striker, Cecil L., Doğan Kuban, and Albrecht Berger. 1997–2007. *Kalenderhane in Istanbul: Final Reports on the Archaeological Exploration and Restoration at Kalenderhane Camii 1966–1978*. 2 vols. Mainz: Verlag Philipp von Zabern.

Strothmann, Werner, ed. 1976. *Drei Gedichte über den Apostel Thomas in Indien*. Göttinger Orientforschungen, Reihe 1, Syriaca 12. Wiesbaden: Harrassowitz.

Szövérffy, J. 1963. "'Peccatrix quondam femina': A Survey of the Mary Magdalen Hymns." *Traditio* 19: 79–146.

Tisserant, E. 1924. "Jacques de Saroug." In *Dictionnaire de Théologie Catholique*, 8.1.300–305. Paris: Letouzey et Ané.

Vööbus, Arthur. 1973–1980. *Handscriftliche Überlieferung der Mēmrē-Dichtung des Ja'qōb von Serūg*. 4 vols. CSCO 344, 345, 421, 422; Subsidia 39, 40, 60, 61. Leuven: CSCO.

Ward, B. 1987. *Harlots of the Desert: A Study of Repentance in Early Monastic Sources*. Kalamazoo, MI: Cistercian Publishing.

Whitby, Mary, and Michael Whitby. 1989. *Chronicon Paschale: 284–628 AD*. Liverpool: Liverpool University Press.

Wellesz, E. 1961. *A History of Byzantine Music and Hymnography*. 2nd ed. Oxford: Clarendon.

Werner, E. 1959–1984. *The Sacred Bridge: The Interdependence of Liturgy and Music in Synagogue and Church during the First Millennium*. New York: Columbia University Press and Ktav Publishing House.

Wigram, W.A. 1929. *The Assyrians and Their Neighbors*. London: Bell.

INDEX

INDEX LOCORUM

Genesis
3:15	80
4:13	28
8:21	72
22	93
22:9	19 n.41

Exodus
15:25	70
30:1	19 n.41
30:7	19 n.41

Joshua
2	108
6	108

2 Samuel
11–12	11, 66

Psalms
51:7	70
103:3	78

Lamentations
3:22–23	82

Isaiah
53:2	18, 74

Hosea
6:6	36

Zechariah
13:7	76

Matthew
5:4	50
5:23	19 n.41
5:29	34
9:9–13	38
9:12–13	36
12:11–12	62
12:43–45	40
13:7	44
14:13–21	38
16:18	70
18:12–14	62
26:6–13	1, 11, 38, 52, 70, 72, 76, 78, 106 n.54
26:31	76
28:18–20	70

Mark
2:13–17	38
4:7	46
6:30–44	38
8:1–10	38
14:3–9	1, 11, 38, 52, 70, 72, 76, 78, 106 n.54

15:40	2	16:32	76
16	2	20	2
		21:25	82

Luke

1:11	19 n.41	*Romans*	
5:27–32	38	5:12–21	80
7:36–50	1, 2, 3, 12, 22 n.46, 38, 44, 52, 54, 56, 58, 60, 62, 64, 66, 68, 96, 104, 106 n.54, 109	*1 Corinthians*	
		9:22	38
		10:33	38
8:2	2	*Ephesians*	
8:7	44	6:16	26
11:24–25	38		
11:37–54	38	*Hebrews*	
15:4–6	62	2:14	80
19:1–10	38	4:14–10:31	54
24	2	7:13	19 n.41
		13:8	82

John

1:5	50, 70	*James*	
3:4	54	2:21	19 n.41
3:17	36		
6:1–13	38	*1 Peter*	
8:12	70	5:8	44
8:15	36		
9:5	70	*Revelation*	
10:1–10	82	6:9	19 n.41
10:11–16	62	8:3	19 n.41
12:1–11	1, 2, 9–10, 11, 52, 54, 72, 76, 106 n.54	22:2	74

INDEX NOMINUM ET RERUM

anoint/anointing   1, 2, 3, 9, 17, 18, 20, 68, 74, 76, 104 n.49, 106, 108
Anastasius I (emperor, 491–518)   4
apostles   1, 3, 11, 18, 70, 72

Amphilochios of Ikonion   103
Arabic   87, 99
arrow/arrows   13, 26, 40
atonement   9, 21–22 n.44, 32, 36, 38, 44, 54, 80, 82
baptism   17–18, 30, 54, 70

Index

Bedjan, Paul 6–7, 8 n.23
Bethany 1, 2 n.3
blemish/blemishes (see *wound/wounds/wounded*)
bow (see *arrow/arrows*)
Christology 3 n.4, 101
Chrysostom, John 5 n.11, 6 n.14, 94 n.18
Constantinople 4, 85, 101–102
Coptic 5
cross 2, 16, 17 n.38
cry/crying (see *weep/weeping*)
dark/darkness 48, 50, 52, 70
David 11, 21–23, 66, 95, 109
debate 4, 20, 88–89, 92, 94–95, 97–98, 98–110, 111
debt/debtor 3, 10, 15–16, 22, 62, 64, 78, 94, 96
demon/demons (see *Satan*)
denarii (see *money*)
devil/devils (see *Satan*)
dialogue (see *debate*)
disciples (see *apostles*)
dispute (see *debate*)
doctor (see *physician*)
eagle 13, 70, 107
Edessa 4
Emesa 4, 85
Ephrem 4–5, 6–8, 10, 12, 12–14, 15 n.34, 16 n.37, 23, 85–86, 86–88, 88–97, 99, 104–110, 110–111
forgiveness 8, 11, 13–14, 15–16, 22, 26, 28, 30, 32, 36, 38, 40, 42, 44, 46, 52, 54, 56, 68, 70, 78, 80, 82, 96, 108
fragrance (see *perfume*)
hair 2, 3, 11, 54, 66, 68
Hannah 109
heal/healing/healed 10 n.27, 21–22, 26, 28, 30, 32, 34, 36, 44, 52, 60, 78, 82, 104
hidden (see *secret/secrecy*)
hunt/hunting 8–9, 13, 26, 40–46, 66, 107
incense 9, 18–19, 21–22, 44, 72, 74
Judas Iscariot 1, 2, 9–10, 11–12, 20, 72, 76
Justinian (emperor, 527–565) 4
kiss/kissing 2–3, 52, 68, 80, 104 n.49
kontakion, genre/form 4–5 n.10, 14, 86, 89–91, 93, 103–105, 110
Lazarus 2
light 34, 48, 50, 52, 70
liturgy/liturgical 4, 17–18, 24, 97–98, 100–101
madrasha/madrashe 14, 88–90, 99
Mary Magdalene 2, 26
Mary, Virgin mother of Jesus 6 n.18, 101 n.39, 102 n.40
medicine/medication/medical (see *physician*)
memra, genre/form 88–90, 97–98, 99
  of Ephrem/attributed to Ephrem 4, 8, 10, 13–14, 23, 86–88, 88–97, 99 n.29, 104–110, 110–111
  of Jacob of Sarug/attributed to Jacob 4, 6–12, 13–14, 14–24, 86, 105 n.52, 106
mercy (see *forgiveness*)
Michal 95, 109
money 1, 2, 3, 11, 76
Nathan 11, 66
Nineveh/Ninevites 21–22
oil 1, 3, 9, 10, 11, 17–20, 22,

30, 44, 52, 54, 68, 70, 72–80
perfume   1, 2, 3, 9, 11–12, 17–18, 21, 46, 52, 68, 72–80, 91–92, 94–97, 104–106, 108
perfume-seller   8–9, 12, 91, 94–97, 106, 108
Peter   21–23
physician   15, 20, 22, 28, 32, 34, 36, 44, 46, 52, 60, 78, 82, 96 n.23, 104–105
Proklos of Constantinople   101–102
prophet/prophecy   3, 11, 56, 58, 60, 62, 66
repentance   8–9, 11, 13–14, 15, 20–23, 26, 30, 32, 42, 46, 50, 58, 80, 86, 87, 94, 96, 107
Rahab   100, 108–109
Romanos the Melode   4–6, 8, 11–12, 14–23, 23–24, 85–111
Satan   2, 4, 7 n.20, 10 n.27, 12–13, 23, 40, 46, 87, 96, 97–110
secret/secrecy   32, 58, 60, 64, 78, 80, 96, 108

silver   (see *money*)
Simon the Leper/Simon the Pharisee   1, 2–4, 8–9, 10, 11, 12, 15, 40, 42, 56, 58, 60, 62–72, 96, 104 n.49
sin/sins   3, 13, 17, 22, 26, 28, 30, 32, 34, 36, 40, 42, 44, 46, 48, 66, 68, 70, 80, 94, 96, 105–106
soghitha/soghyatha   4, 12–14, 23, 86, 88–89 n.7, 96, 97–110, 110–111
smoke   (see *incense*)
tears   (see *weep/weeping*)
trap/trapping   (see *hunt/hunting*)
water   3, 17, 30, 54, 66
weep/weeping   2–3, 9, 11, 17, 14, 21–23, 26, 30, 34, 36, 44, 46, 50, 52, 54, 56, 66, 68, 70, 80, 82, 96, 109
wound/wounds/wounded   14, 22, 28, 32, 34, 36, 38, 44, 46, 50, 52, 58, 68, 78, 104

www.ingramcontent.com/pod-product-compliance
Lightning Source LLC
Chambersburg PA
CBHW020656300426
44112CB00007B/400